Winston Churchill

the Photobiography

Winston
Churchill
the Photobiography

Michael Paterson

Pictures edited by Neil Baber and Michael Paterson

D&C
David and Charles

A DAVID & CHARLES BOOK
Copyright © David & Charles Limited 2006

David & Charles is an F+W Publications Inc. company
4700 East Galbraith Road, Cincinnati, OH 45236

First published in the UK in 2006

Text copyright © Michael Paterson 2006
Photographs copyright © Mirrorpix 2006 except those listed on page 204.

Michael Paterson has asserted his right to be identified as author of this work
in accordance with the Copyright, Designs and Patents Act, 1988.

A catalogue record for this book is available from the British Library.
ISBN-13: 978-0-7153-2312-0
ISBN-10: 0-7153-2312-1

Printed in China by SNP Leefung
for David & Charles   Brunel House   Newton Abbot   Devon

Commissioning Editor   Neil Baber
Editor   Ame Verso
Art Editor   Mike Moule
Design Assistants   Sarah Clark & Emma Sandquest
Production Controller   Kelly Smith

Visit our website at www.davidandcharles.co.uk

David & Charles books are available from all good bookshops; alternatively you can contact our
Orderline on 0870 9908222 or write to us at FREEPOST EX2 110, D&C Direct, Newton Abbot, TQ12 4ZZ
(no stamp required UK only); US customers call 800-289-0963 and Canadian customers call 800-840-5220.

CONTENTS

INTRODUCTION

More than 40 years after his death, the worldwide fascination with Sir Winston Churchill shows no sign of abating. His face is more instantly recognizable to an international public than that of most present-day politicians. His personal accoutrements – the cigar and siren suit – are, like his V-for-victory sign, at once identifiable even to those with little knowledge of British history. The majority of his numerous books remain in print and are admired for the quality of their writing, while his speeches are frequently quoted, broadcast and anthologized. More than 1000 books have been written about him, some dealing with aspects as specific as his bouts of depression or his sense of humour. He has been the subject of films and a stage musical, as well as a multitude of television documentaries and dramatizations. There are monuments to him in places as disparate as Quebec and Quito, and his picture appears on the stamps of several countries that he never visited. Objects ranging from a railway engine to a rhododendron have been named after him. Museums and collections from Bletchley to Brunei bear witness to the vast amount of memorabilia that has celebrated his life and achievements since he first came to public notice as an author in the late 1890s. The cult of Churchill provides continuing proof that 'heroes belong to the world'.

Why, in an era of short memory and impatience with hagiography, is this British politician still so revered? That question can be answered on several levels. All his admirers are agreed that his defiance of Hitler during the summer of 1940 was one of history's great acts of courage. German armies had conquered the whole of Europe, and British troops had only just been saved from capture at Dunkirk. Britain and her Commonwealth were in no position to take on the might of Hitler's legions, and there was no visible prospect of assistance from other powerful nations; the United States was apparently committed to neutrality and the Soviet Union – the only other superpower – had recently made an alliance with Germany.

As well as the threat of attack, Churchill faced the temptation of an easy option – negotiation with Hitler. The reason for Britain's declaration of war – the occupation of Poland – was no longer an issue. Hitler, a professed Anglophile, made clear his willingness to leave the United Kingdom alone in return for the freedom to pursue his designs on the European continent. Some of Churchill's colleagues, and a section of public opinion, favoured coming to terms. Churchill knew, however, that to treat with the Führer would be fatal to Britain's future security. His refusal even to consider compromising with Hitler was seen by the British people as the right choice, even though it meant years of terrible hardship and loss. This stubbornness, and the resulting Battle of Britain, were the first defeats to be suffered by Hitler, and gave hope to millions that German victory was not inevitable. By keeping the European conflict going until it widened into a world war (and Hitler's mistakes brought both America and Russia into the Allied camp), Churchill ensured the defeat of the Axis. He thus became an international symbol of freedom and of the triumph of democracy over totalitarianism, and this is how he continues to be remembered.

In addition to this semi-mythical status, Churchill is seen as a man of great and varied gifts – a latter-day renaissance prince. He was a Nobel Prize-winning author, and a distinguished politician who won votes for over 60 years and held almost all Cabinet positions (he served in every post except that of Foreign Secretary). He was a talented painter, a witty and erudite speaker, a fearless and enterprising soldier, a tireless traveller, an enthusiastic sportsman and a devoted family man. His personality also gives evidence of quirky and unexpected traits – such as his fondness for butterflies or his skill at brick-laying – that make the study of his life a pleasurable voyage of discovery. Add to this his all-too-human delight in food, alcohol, good talk and luxury, and he emerges as an endearing figure whose appetite for life many people envy. Whether as a statesman, a writer or merely as someone who got the utmost out of his circumstances, Churchill's life, as well as his achievement, is thus an inspiration.

For those impressed by determination, Churchill's immense willpower provides an uplifting example. Though he came from a background of social privilege, he had to struggle to enter his chosen field of politics. He acquired through his own efforts – long hours spent studying topical issues and parliamentary debates – the equivalent of a university education, and over-came both a speech impediment and an inability to speak spontaneously to become, eventually, the most accomplished orator in the House of Commons. As a soldier, he lobbied exhaustively to take part in military expeditions and dangerous fighting, and showed conspicuous bravery on the battlefield.

As a politician promoted rapidly to major government office, Churchill's rise to greatness abruptly ended in 1915 when he was blamed for the failure of the Allied landings at Gallipoli. He lost his position as First Lord of the Admiralty, and there seemed little prospect of him holding power again. In the event, he was back in the government two years later, but this spell in the wilderness was to be repeated in the 1930s, when once again he was written off as a spent force. He had, during his career in Parliament, provoked the virulent animosity of influential MPs, and his years out of office were no doubt rendered more bitter by the barely disguised glee of his enemies. Yet his sense of destiny and of his own fitness to direct the course of events never wavered, no matter how discouraging the political or international climate. In May 1940, when World War II began in earnest, he was 65 – too old, in the view of many, to take on the stress and responsibility of the premiership. Though in retrospect he seems the obvious choice to lead the nation's war effort, at the time there was widespread distrust and suspicion. He was perceived as unstable, his record in the previous conflict suggested bad judgment and costly mistakes, and he was thought to be a heavy drinker. Those who regarded him as unsuitable included some of his closest friends.

Churchill quickly proved his detractors wrong. His spirit of implacable determination inspired the British people and carried them with him through the years that followed, despite the Blitz and a series of initial military reverses. By the war's end he was, of course, a national hero, but the public felt he was not a suitable Prime Minister for the new era and his Labour opponents decisively won the general election of July 1945. Aged 70 and exhausted by the burden he had borne, he had had no thought of relinquishing power, and saw his rejection at the polls as an act of terrible ingratitude. Though his wife Clementine hoped that he would retire gracefully and spend his remaining years enjoying the plaudits he had earned, he was determined to wipe out the humiliation of defeat by winning the premiership again. For this reason he refused to hand over the leadership of the Conservative Party to his young, able heir-assumptive, Anthony Eden. His persistence paid off when, in October 1951, he once again became Prime Minister, at 77. In spite of debilitating strokes, he remained in office until his 81st year, resigning in April 1955. Still refusing to retire, he continued to be a Member of Parliament, albeit an increasingly inactive one, until September 1964, when he was almost 90. Through a combination of overwhelming force of will and unremitting energy, Churchill had built the career of which, as a young man, he had dreamed, though he bore it on to heights that even his exceptional self-confidence could surely not have envisaged.

Churchill's character, like his career, compels our interest. Though he became in later life a symbol of Britain, there was little about him that conformed to the stereotypes of Anglo-Saxon behaviour. Nor was he in any sense a typical member of the patrician caste into which he was born. He was highly emotional and easily moved to tears. Though he could be extremely charming when he chose, he was guilty at all stages of his life of thoughtless and often striking rudeness (excused by some commentators as the behaviour of a 'natural aristocrat'). He was not a man of Olympian calm – his tantrums and sulks are well documented by those who worked for him, though they usually blew over and were forgotten fairly quickly, and he could apologize graciously afterwards to whoever had been on the receiving end. He was largely a stranger to modesty and he made no effort, when young, to conceal or play down his overwhelming desire to succeed. He had none of the studied languor – the attempt to make achievement look effort-less – that often characterizes the products of public schools. He was intensely industrious, armed with formidable powers of concentration and capable of dealing with mountains of paperwork – or producing thousands of words for his books – in the course of a day. He cut his days in half by taking a (very un-British) siesta, which gave him sufficient energy to carry on working until the early hours. By this means – and with the help of a staff of secretaries and researchers – he was able to produce a virtually endless stream of articles, books and letters.

If he was not a typical product of his country, it is equally true that Churchill was not typical of his time. When he entered Parliament at the age of 26 in 1901, it was said of him by a journalist that 'He has the 20th century in his marrow.' This was, however, never true. His attitudes and his nature were formed by the era into which he had been born – the high noon of Victorian aristocratic confidence – and he remained part of that world all his life. His attachment to this period was a matter of both sentimental inclination and deliberate choice. 'I like to live in the past,' he was to say during the 1950s, 'I don't think people are going to get much fun in the future.' Though his financial fortunes waxed and waned, he was never without a staff of servants, including a valet to run his twice-daily baths, to lay out his clothes (he changed his shirt several times a day) and to tie his famous polka-dot bow ties. He did not carry money, did not go into shops and had no idea how to use public transport (he once, famously, had to be rescued from the London Underground because he couldn't get off). When, setting out on journeys, he wanted to know if his car was ready, he had a habit of asking: 'Is the coachman on his box?'

He was in no sense a 'man of the people' and, despite his popular wartime image as 'Good Old Winnie', he had nothing in common with the working classes. Although he had had an interest in social reform during his years in a Liberal government before World War I, he knew little about the lives of ordinary voters. His use, when Home Secretary in 1911, of soldiers to quell industrial unrest made him a hate figure to many socialists, as did his unwise policies when Chancellor of the Exchequer, which led, in 1926, to the General Strike. Only his World War II apotheosis went some way toward altering this image.

Churchill's preference was for the rich. He had aristocratic tastes and was incapable of economy. His country house, Chartwell, proved beyond his means to keep up (it was eventually bought for him by admirers). He had to pay for servants, travel, immense repasts, champagne and cigars, and, although he was well paid as a writer, journalist and cabinet minister, he was in debt for most of his adult life. His friends – Lord Beaverbrook, Sir Ernest Cassell, Aristotle Onassis and others – helped him to live the life he both craved and expected from fate. Only when his post-war writing made him a millionaire did he join the ranks of the wealthy in his own right.

His friends were not, of course, all plutocrats. The varied roles he played in the course of his life – parliamentarian, author, soldier and latterly world leader – meant that, for six decades of the 20th century, he met or had dealings with almost everyone who mattered. He knew not only Josef Stalin and Charles de Gaulle but also Rupert Brooke and Laurence Olivier.

Churchill's public life began at almost exactly the moment that newspapers began to publish photographs. His controversial, colourful career ensured that public interest in him did not flag, and as the decades passed the files on him in newspaper archives expanded. When he graduated from national to international celebrity after 1940, the demand for pictures of him increased even further. Not all of them have survived, for lack of sentiment – or lack of space – has led some archivists to consign these images to oblivion. Those that remain, such as the Mirrorpix collection, which comprises the archives of the *Daily Mirror*, *Daily Record* and *Daily Herald* newspapers among others, form a delightful treasure house of Churchilliana, chronicling his life from his infancy and schooldays until the moment his coffin was borne up the River Thames on its journey to Bladon churchyard. The pictures that follow – some well known and others virtually unknown – have been chosen to offer a balance between the different aspects of their subject: the young and the old, the public and the private, the active and the thoughtful, the solemn and the humorous. Together, they form a unique record of a unique individual.

Chapter 1: EARLY LIFE 1874–1900

Winston Churchill was born, on 30 November 1874, into a family that was not only great but also famous. That is, his forebears were dukes while his parents were celebrities. His father, Lord Randolph, was a political rising star who seemed to many an almost inevitable future Prime Minister. His mother, the American Jennie Jerome, was one of the greatest beauties in London society and was alleged to be a former lover of the Prince of Wales. Though not wealthy – at least by comparison with much of the aristocracy – the Churchills were popular and moved in fashionable circles. They knew the leading personalities in politics, the arts, the services and finance. They belonged to a caste that took power and influence for granted.

Winston's formative years therefore endowed him with an unbreakable self-confidence. On visits to Blenheim Palace, his family's imposing country house in Oxfordshire, he would have absorbed the sense of power and tradition that was his birth-right. In his parents' home he would have grown up surrounded by the sophisticated talk of social and political insiders. This meant that he was unusually well informed for his age and that he had no qualms about talking to adults on equal terms – characteristics that were noticed, and admired, by those who met him. Many of these predicted a bright future for him.

In 1882 he was sent away to begin his education. He attended two preparatory schools before entering Harrow at the age of 14. It has been suggested by many biographers – and by Churchill himself – that his schooldays were unremittingly miserable and that he showed no promise, but this is inaccurate. He undoubtedly received punishments, though these were not for inability but for impertinence. His academic record at Harrow was satisfactory and he won several prizes – testimony to both his emerging skill in writing and his powerful memory. A naturally weak child, he also had some success as an athlete, excelling in swimming and becoming, in 1892, Public Schools Fencing Champion.

Churchill's early life was defined by two things – his feelings toward his father and his sense of his own destiny. He viewed Lord Randolph – a somewhat distant and preoccupied parent – with uncritical admiration. His great ambition was to follow his father into politics and work beside him. Lord Randolph, however, resigned from office in 1886, and gradually fell victim to an illness that killed him at the age of 46, while his son was a military cadet. The effect of Lord Randolph's death was to spur Winston to vindicate his memory and to carry on his interrupted political career by achieving high office. It also suggested that Winston too might live only until his mid-40s. This sense of doom was the reason he was in such a hurry to make his mark.

From his schooldays onward, he frankly told those around him that destiny had great things in store for him. Confident young men frequently say this type of thing, but Churchill had about him – though physically he was not in the least prepossessing – a distinct 'presence' that seemed to mark him out. He once told a senior boy who was caning him: 'I will be a greater man than you!'

In 1893 he entered the Royal Military College at Sandhurst. This focused his energies and, for the first time, enabled him to achieve outright excellence. Passing out among the highest-scoring cadets, he joined a smart cavalry unit, the 4th Hussars. He was, however, impatient to get on in the world, and quickly realized that life in a regiment on peacetime garrison duty would mean wasting several years. Seeking excitement, in 1895 he therefore spent his leave visiting Cuba, where a war was being fought between the Spanish Army and indigenous rebels. He accompanied the troops for several days as a military observer, experienced action for the first time, and had his account of the campaign published in newspapers. He had successfully adopted the dual role of soldier and writer.

Through the following years he developed this with great success. He got himself attached to an expedition to India's North-West Frontier, saw some fighting, and wrote his first book, *The Malakand Field Force*. The next year, 1898, his mother's formidable range of influential friendships gained him access to a major campaign in the Sudan, where forces commanded by Lord Kitchener defeated Muslim extremists in a decisive battle at Omdurman. Having beaten the odds to be there, Churchill took part in a cavalry charge, in which he survived savage fighting. He also wrote another book.

Throughout his formative years Churchill made use of every possible contact that he felt would be helpful – his father's old colleagues, his mother's old lovers, and anyone else who could be persuaded to support him. He appreciated to the full the advantage that these friendships brought (later in life he would try to help others in the same way), but justified them with characteristic eloquence as providing 'a springboard, not a sofa' – he looked for opportunities for responsibility and service, not a comfortable sinecure based on his social status.

He had now acquired the glory and reputation he had sought as a prelude to a political life, and wished to enter Parliament. He lost an election at Oldham in Lancashire, but gained a respectable share of the vote. Within months, however, he was involved in another military campaign. The Boer War (1899–1902) was fought between British forces and the citizen armies of two Dutch-speaking South African republics. While Britain could field larger numbers, the Boers possessed greater skill and, in some cases, better weapons, and the contest became a humiliation for Britain. Churchill, now a professional journalist, travelled to the scene of action and, while on patrol with troops, was captured, but broke out of prison and escaped from enemy territory. This event made headlines around the world, and he became a popular hero in Britain.

After rejoining the army for several months, he returned to England to prepare for a career in public service. Members of Parliament received no salary at that time, and he had no expectations from his father's estate. He made up for this by undertaking a lucrative lecture tour of North America and by further writing. In October 1900 he stood, once again, as a Conservative candidate in the seat of Oldham. This time he won.

Winston with his mother, Ireland, 1876.

Victorian children of all classes – and both sexes – wore dresses until the age of three, and boys did not have their hair cut until about the same age. One of the sandy curls that Winston is sporting is now preserved in the room in which he was born at Blenheim Palace.

Harrow School register of new boys, 1888.

Winston's arrival, at the age of 14, was recorded in April 1888. Interestingly, another boy listed on the same page, Campbell-Colquohoun, gives his address as Chartwell, Westerham, Kent. In 1922 Churchill was to buy the house from this family, which had owned it since the mid-19th century.

In his school uniform, Harrow School, 1889.

Winston as a 15-year-old schoolboy, dressed in the Eton collar and short jacket of a junior boy. He was small and stocky in build with a snub nose, blue eyes and a crooked mouth. His red hair made him as conspicuous in the school as his noisy self-confidence.

Lady Randolph Churchill with her two sons, Winston and Jack, London, 1889.

Winston's brother was five years his junior, and entirely different in personality – quiet, studious and thoughtful. The two boys were to share a room at Harrow. Both at school and throughout his later life, Jack was to be overwhelmed, and overshadowed, by his famous brother.

Winston's mother, the daughter of a flamboyant New York financier, was renowned for her beauty and wit. During his childhood, he recalled, 'I loved her dearly but at a distance.' This image of her as aloof and unapproachable is greatly exaggerated: from the time he entered the adult world, she made persistent efforts to further his career. Using her network of social contacts, she got him into his chosen regiment,

found publishers for his books and introduced him to senior officers who could grant him permission to take part in military campaigns.

Outgoing, adventurous and determined, it was from her that Winston inherited the characteristics that made him successful – energy, ambition and a refusal to give up. Though he modelled himself on his father, it was his mother who shaped his personality.

With fellow officer cadets at the Royal Military
College, Sandhurst, 1893–4.

Winston gained entry to the Royal Military College
on his third attempt – competition was so fierce that
this was no disgrace – and arrived there in September
1893. He wrote: 'I am very contented and like the place
very much.' He excelled in Topography, Fortification,
Tactics, Riding, Drill and Military Law, but was not a
noticeably smart cadet – in this photograph one of
his uniform buttons is undone.

In the dress uniform of the 4th Hussars, Aldershot, 1894.

From the Royal Military College, Churchill entered the cavalry, the most fashionable and expensive arm of service. The 4th Hussars, raised in 1658, had a distinguished record and a splendid uniform – a dark blue tunic and breeches with gold braid and frogging, and a sealskin busby with a high scarlet plume. Tailored to make the stocky young man seem tall and slim, this was bought on credit. It was so expensive that by the time he had paid for it, six years later, he had left the Army.

Wearing the frock coat and pillbox hat of a cavalry officer, Aldershot, 1894.

Churchill took his regimental duties seriously but found little stimulation in garrison life. Looking for advancement and adventure, in December 1895 he used his leave to visit Cuba and observe Spanish troops fighting local insurgents. This provided his first taste of action, his first medal, and his first published writing.

In khaki service dress outside the bungalow he
shared with other officers, Bangalore, India, 1897.

The 4th Hussars were posted to India, but Churchill
found useful ways to escape the boredom of routine.
As well as playing polo and reading voraciously, he
succeeded in getting attached to punitive expeditions
and took part in fighting in Malakand and the Sudan.
He wrote accounts of both these campaigns, based
on his newspaper dispatches, which sold well and
established his literary reputation.

Churchill the civilian war correspondent, with British troops in South Africa, 1899.

By this time an author of experience and proven ability, Churchill meticulously planned his journey to South Africa. With him went practical clothing, extensive supplies of wine and whisky, his Army pistol – and his valet. He also equipped himself with letters of introduction; for the book he intended to write on the war, he would provide not only background detail and first-hand accounts, but interviews with as many of the principal figures in the conflict as he could obtain.

A studio portrait of the ambitious young politician and author, taken shortly after his arrival in South Africa, 1899.

Churchill did not want a career in the Army. His desire was to win fame as a soldier and writer, then enter politics. Though he had managed to gain the reputation he had sought and resigned his commission to pursue his political ambitions, he lost his first election at Oldham in Lancashire. The outbreak of war in South Africa offered the prospect of well-paid journalism and he returned to the world of military action, though this time as an outsider.

Returning from South Africa a hero, 1899.

Unable to resist the prospect of action, Churchill took part in a patrol and was captured. Treated as a combatant and imprisoned, he escaped by climbing over the wall of the compound. He travelled for days through enemy territory, hiding in goods wagons and – with the help of a sympathetic British national – taking refuge in a mine shaft. His safe arrival in Portuguese East Africa made him a hero. This photograph was taken on board a steamer travelling from Lourenço Marques (now Maputo) to Durban. Churchill was clearly enjoying not only his freedom but also the attention his daring exploits had brought him.

Chapter 2: **RADICAL POLITICS 1900–1911**

Churchill started his political career in the year that the 20th century began. He entered the Commons in the first weeks of 1901, at the age of 26. His fame as a soldier, a writer and the son of a famous father meant that he had no need to serve an apprenticeship in obscurity. He believed, in any case, that his background had given him sufficient political education and that he did not need the guidance of senior Conservatives.

In his maiden speech he plunged into a debate about the very subject – the 'Army Estimates', or defence budget – that had caused Lord Randolph to resign a quarter of a century earlier. To his listeners he sounded – and to some extent looked – like a reincarnation of his father. The oratorical style, the forward-stooping stance and other mannerisms were strikingly similar – as they should have been, for he had deliberately copied them. He had also studied Lord Randolph's speeches and committed many of them to memory, and in 1906 he published a biography of his father that was predictably hero-worshipping in tone. As for a style of his own, he was a powerful but not a natural speaker, and was easily flustered by interruptions. He would memorize his speeches and practise their delivery in front of a mirror. He worked, relentlessly but unsuccessfully, to eliminate a slight speech impediment.

Another thing Churchill had adopted from his father was the principle of 'Tory Democracy', a somewhat opportunistic espousal of the common man as a source of Conservative votes. Though he was committed to this for sentimental reasons he was, in addition, a politician who refused to compromise his personal convictions for the sake of party unity. These attitudes put him on the left of his party, made him a nuisance to diehard Conservatives and meant that on many issues he had more in common with the opposition than with the government. In May 1904, having decided that the issue of free trade (favoured by him and by the Liberals) versus protectionism (the Conservative stance) put too much of a strain on his loyalty, he resigned from his party and joined the opposition.

This was seen by many as a cynical career move. The Conservative Party was led by an older generation, and there seemed little opportunity for advancement. Public opinion was in any case tiring of the government, and it did Churchill's prospects no harm to align himself with the probable future rulers. In 1906 the Liberals won power, and the next year he entered the Cabinet for the first time as Undersecretary of State for the Colonies. Because his superior, the kindly and introverted Earl of Elgin, sat in the Lords, it fell to Churchill to represent his department in the Commons, and he thus became de facto a major member of the government. He went on to serve as President of the Board of Trade (effectively secretary of state for commerce) in 1908 and Home Secretary (1910). This was a remarkably swift rise to one of the most important posts in government. Despite an often rude and bumptious exterior, Churchill possessed undoubted abilities. He had a formidable capacity for work and an impressive command of detail. His manner often irritated those who worked for him, but his departments got through a great deal of business. He was interested in all aspects of government, and had no qualms about interfering wherever he saw fit. Opinion within Whitehall and Parliament divided on whether he was a blessing or a curse.

Churchill was not afraid of unpopularity, and this was just as well, for he aroused considerable ire across the political spectrum. His desertion to the Liberals earned the lasting hatred of his erstwhile colleagues, and his enthusiasm in pursuing anti-aristocratic measures damned him as a traitor in the eyes of his own class. (For a time, he was persona non grata in every country house in Britain, except for his cousin's home at Blenheim). His opposition to votes for women made him a hate-figure to suffragettes. As Home Secretary, his ready use of massed police and troops to combat strikes smacked, to active socialists, of the methods of tsarist Russia.

His career had for years been characterized by a determination to achieve office. With no capacity for small talk and no interest in social trivialities, there had been few opportunities to seek a wife. He had, however, on three occasions gone as far as proposing. The first young woman, Pamela Plowden, had caught his eye in India. The second was the actress Ethel Barrymore and the third a shipping heiress, Muriel Wilson. Though his aura of power and ambition may have exerted fascination, his extravagance, mercurial nature and obsession with his future perhaps suggested that he would be too difficult to live with.

The woman he married in 1908, Clementine Hozier, had herself twice broken off engagements. She came from a staunchly Liberal family and had political views that would often be at odds with those of her husband. Though she was not wealthy and brought no financial stability (at that time MPs received no salary) she provided more important things – a seemingly endless tolerance of his moods, preoccupations and raffish friends, and a stable home environment. Despite her own intelligence, their marriage was not a union of equals, for her life was to be subsumed in his career. She consciously decided to put his happiness before that of herself or their children.

Churchill became Home Secretary in January 1910. At 36, he was the youngest holder of the office since Robert Peel. He had earned a reputation as a radical and had developed an effective working relationship with the Chancellor of the Exchequer, David Lloyd George. He was therefore deeply involved in the 'Peoples' Budget', which laid the foundations of the welfare state. He was instrumental in introducing the old age pension and he established Britain's first Labour Exchanges.

The most enduring image of Churchill as Home Secretary was provided, in January 1911, by the 'Siege of Sidney Street'. A group of armed foreign anarchists barricaded themselves in a house in London's East End, surrounded by soldiers and police. Churchill rushed to the scene and, when the house caught fire, ordered firemen not to risk their lives by intervening. The culprits perished. His presence at this event was widely regarded as interfering, irresponsible, vainglorious and immature – but he relished the adventure and said afterwards 'It was such fun.'

The new Member of Parliament for Oldham, 1900.

Home from the Boer War, Churchill received several offers to represent constituencies as their MP. He returned to Oldham, and won the seat by over 200 votes. Memories of his father were still fresh in the Commons, and the similarity between his manner and outlook and that of Lord Randolph delighted some and horrified others. As can be seen in this picture he had already, at the start of his career, adopted the square-topped bowler hat that was to remain a trademark throughout World War II. This style, called a 'Cambridge', gave him greater height, though as the years went by it made him look increasingly old-fashioned.

Daily Mirror

THE MORNING JOURNAL WITH THE SECOND LARGEST NET SALE.

ASK FOR the Special Extra
BEAUTY NUMBER
of the "DAILY MIRROR."
PRICE ONE PENNY.
NOW ON SALE.

No. 1,414. Registered at the G. P. O. as a Newspaper.   MONDAY, MAY 11, 1908.   One Halfpenny.

MR. WINSTON CHURCHILL FINDS "A SAFE SEAT" AT LAST: REJECTED IN MANCHESTER, HE IS ELECTED M.P. FOR DUNDEE.

Amid scenes of tremendous excitement Mr. Winston Churchill was declared member for Dundee on Saturday night, having polled 2,709 more votes than Sir George Baxter, the Unionist candidate. The Liberal majority, however, is practically only half what it was at the general election, when Mr. E. Robertson polled 5,411 more votes than the Unionist. In the photograph Mr. Churchill is acknowledging the cheers of his supporters.—(*Daily Mirror* photograph.)

The *Daily Mirror* marks Churchill's election to a safe seat after several turbulent years in his political career, Dundee, 1908.

Having sensationally changed parties in 1904, Churchill was appointed by the Liberal Prime Minister, H.H. Asquith, to the post of President of the Board of Trade in April 1908. This involved him having to seek re-election, and he suffered defeat at the hands of a Conservative. A safe seat had to be found for him quickly, and the following month he secured the diehard Liberal constituency of Dundee in Scotland. His ministerial career saved after an embarrassing upset, he could look forward to further political glory.

Churchill with his American cousin by marriage,
Consuela, Duchess of Marlborough, Blenheim
Palace, 1904.

Like his mother, Consuela was a wealthy American
(in her case, a Vanderbilt) who had married into the
British aristocracy. The relationship ended in divorce
and with her second husband, a Frenchman, she
went to live abroad, though she and Churchill
remained lifelong friends. This photograph
was probably taken while he was working, in
the Blenheim archives, on his biography of his
father, Lord Randolph.

The young politician, Dundee, *c.*1907.

Churchill excited interest and controversy during his early years in Parliament. He changed parties, became increasingly radical, and began his ascent toward high office when appointed Undersecretary of State for the Colonies. Lord Elgin, who presided over the department, said of him: 'He is most tiresome to deal with and will, I fear, give trouble.'

Having left the Conservatives for the Liberals in 1904, he gained the lasting hatred of the Tories, who dubbed him 'the Blenheim Rat'. His switch of allegiance was the beginning of a reputation for mercurial instability that lasted for decades.

This image captures the thrusting energy of the young Churchill, expressed in his purposeful stride, and his look of fierce concentration.

Portrait with Astrakhan-collared coat, 1900.

Churchill cultivated a number of idiosyncrasies throughout his career in public life. One of the first was this coat, a style not considered altogether reputable.

He would become best known, however, for his hats. He had a large head, and went prematurely bald. When he once accidentally put on a hat that was too small, cariacaturists seized on it and it became his trademark.

On the election campaign trail, Manchester, 1908.
Churchill was a naturally poor speaker who
worked exhaustively to improve his style, but whose
quick-thinking wit was usually more than a match
for hecklers. He made a number of enemies from
the start of his career, and in the politically turbulent
years prior to World War I perhaps the most vociferous
were the proponents of votes for women. Here he
was campaigning in a crowded Manchester street.
His audience listened politely, but he was to lose the
election. Despite a lengthy career as an MP, he was
to suffer several such defeats.

Interrupted by a suffragette while addressing factory workers in their lunch hour, Dundee, 1908.

As Home Secretary, Churchill was ultimately responsible for the force-feeding of suffragettes on hunger strike in prison. He was also blamed for alleged police brutality toward protesters during a suffrage demonstration in London in November 1910 – as a result of this he was attacked by a male sympathizer.

He had already, in the previous year, been assaulted with a whip by a woman at Bristol railway station. Clementine, who was strongly in favour of the granting of votes to women, had to suppress her own feelings to support her husband. Their children Diana (born in 1909) and Randolph (1911) were threatened with kidnap, and, when taken on their daily walks by nannies, had to have police protection.

Mr and Mrs Churchill, Westminster, 1908.

Churchill's wedding to Clementine Hozier in September 1908 was a major 'media event'. Held at St Margaret's, Westminster, the most fashionable church in London, it was attended by much of the political establishment. Despite his desertion of the Conservative Party four years earlier, one of his former colleagues, Lord Hugh Cecil, acted as best man. With the preoccupation that had always been one of his most prominent characteristics, Churchill was found deep in political discussion in the church vestry only minutes before the ceremony. His wife Clementine, who shared the Liberal beliefs that he was at the time espousing, fortunately possessed a high tolerance level. She would need it in the years ahead.

Clementine Hozier and Winston Churchill, 1908.
   This contemporary composite photograph, stitched
together from two separate portraits, is testament to
public interest in the match at the time.

In the uniform of a Privy Councillor, London, 1907.

Churchill loved dressing up, and perhaps no country could better indulge him by offering such a range of official uniforms. In 1907, at the age of 32, he became a member of the Privy Council. This select body of advisers to the sovereign dates from the Middle Ages. Its regular meetings are always conducted standing up, as a means of hastening business. The dark blue uniform seen here, with its gold braid and cocked hat, is in fact the less splendid of two that are worn by members. The man to the right of Churchill, with scarlet tunic and swan feather-plumed helmet, belongs to an equally ancient and splendid organization – the Honourable Corps of Gentlemen at Arms. Composed of retired officers, it attends the monarch on state occasions.

Presented at court, London, 1908.

Churchill and his Cabinet colleague, Sir John Morley, arrive at St James's Palace to attend a levee, wearing the 'levee dress' of Privy Councillors. St James's was, and is, the setting for numerous court and diplomatic events. Levees, which were held regularly, were presentations to the monarch of government officials, service officers, prominent citizens and important foreign visitors. Participants filed in line past the King, held a brief conversation, and left.

With the Kaiser, Germany, 1906.

On two occasions within four years, Churchill was invited to attend the autumn manoeuvres of the German armies as a guest of Kaiser Wilhelm II. These were colossal displays of military might by the most formidable power in Continental Europe, and Churchill found the spectacle both impressive and deeply disturbing. He knew, however, that for all their splendour and discipline the German forces lacked the vital experience of actual warfare that their British counterparts had gained through continuous colonial campaigns. This was indeed to give British troops an important edge when conflict broke out in 1914. Churchill wears the uniform of a major in the cavalry.

Observing German Army manoeuvres, 1909.

On his second visit, while watching the German troops parade or advance, Churchill's trained eye noticed the steady modernization of their tactics and weaponry, which he feared would be deployed against Britain within a few years. International tensions were at such a pitch that war could have broken out at any time. Britain was committed by treaty to alliance with France and Russia, while Germany's rapid creation of a large navy threatened Britain's maritime supremacy. Despite the superficial bonhomie of these visits, the two sides were already prepared for the coming showdown. It is often thought that this picture shows Churchill with the Kaiser. In fact, as can be seen from his uniform, this man is not even a Prussian but an infantry officer from the Duchy of Baden.

The Siege of Sidney Street, Stepney, London, 1911.

Churchill presided over the Home Office in an era of turmoil and crisis, dealing with strikes, suffragettes and even international terrorism. His most memorable action as Home Secretary was not his successful introduction of Labour Exchanges but his dramatic arrival at a terrorist incident. Eastern European anarchists, who had carried out robberies and killed three policemen, were cornered in a house in London's East End. Because they were armed, Churchill ordered troops to the scene: Scots Guards and even the Royal Horse Artillery were sent for.

Churchill directs operations in Sidney Street, 1911.

Churchill is in the centre of the picture, dressed in a silk top hat and leaning slightly forwards. When the building where the terrorists were holding out caught fire, Churchill, as the highest official on the scene, took control: he forbade the fire brigade to risk their lives by intervening, and the defenders died. The public and the press were horrified that he had turned a London street into a battlefield. He was to demonstrate a similar attitude to strikers later that year – a resort to force without bothering to negotiate. He was widely criticized and ridiculed – cinema audiences booed his appearance on news-reels – and was obliged to appear before an enquiry.

Chapter 3: **WAR LORD 1911–22**

In October 1911 Churchill was given another, and even more significant, Cabinet post when he became First Lord of the Admiralty. This meant that he was the civilian head of the Royal Navy, at that time one of the largest and most formidable weapons in the world (the others were the German and Russian Armies). For Churchill, fascinated by warfare and with a love of tradition, this was a triumph. The administration of the Navy was the task of the Board of Admiralty, presided over by a senior officer, the First Sea Lord. The First Lord of the Admiralty – a political appointee – represented the service in Parliament and implemented government policy with regard to the Navy. Often this post had been filled by older, more venerable men for whom it was the dignified finale to a career in public life. By Churchill's time, however, the world was too dangerous for the office to be treated as a glittering ornament. Rivalry between the European powers was so great that war was seen as both inevitable and imminent. The Royal Navy, Britain's principal defence, was undergoing rapid modernization under the guidance of two energetic First Sea Lords – Prince Louis of Battenberg (1912–14) and Admiral John 'Jacky' Fisher (1914–15). Churchill's passionate energy, enthusiasm and knowledge were put to use to drive this process on with even greater urgency.

This was the biggest challenge he had faced, and he threw himself into the work with characteristic determination. Making it his business to visit every ship, training facility and shore establishment, he developed a greater knowledge of the service than anyone in Parliament. Working closely with the First Sea Lords, he had warships equipped with more powerful guns, and oversaw their conversion from coal to oil. Seeing the potential of the aircraft in future conflicts, he established the Royal Naval Air Service in 1912. In order to gain experience of the new technology he took flying lessons.

His reforms were only just in time. By the summer of 1914 the German Navy, which had been expanding steadily for more than a decade, had almost reached parity with Britain's fleet. As Europe drifted inexorably into full-scale war, Churchill cancelled the summer leave of sailors and naval reservists following their annual training. This meant that, when hostilities broke out, the Royal Navy was ready to go straight to its war stations before the enemy could attack across the North Sea.

Always a showman, he relished the opportunities offered by the war. Despite the gravity of his responsibilities at the Admiralty, he hastened to Belgium to organize the defence of Antwerp against the German Armies, taking with him a hastily assembled force of sailors and Royal Marines (troops who came under his authority as First Lord), hundreds of whom were half-trained recruits. They fought as soldiers, and suffered heavy casualties, but Antwerp was lost and Churchill's credibility suffered. His actions suggested to the public, and to military commanders, that his only interest was in personal glory.

As the war settled into stalemate and it became evident that neither side could break through the defences of the other, Churchill proposed that an attack be made on Germany's eastern ally – the Ottoman Empire. By capturing the strategically vital Bosphorus and seizing Constantinople, a wedge could be driven through the coalition of enemy nations, Germany could be attacked from the rear and aid could be brought to Russia. As strategy it was sound, but it proved impractical. The proposal was for a naval expedition, but Army involvement and the hasty assembling of a landing force added complications. The naval attack was unsuccessful, and valuable time was lost in deciding how to proceed. By the time an assault began, with inadequate resources, on 25 April 1915, the Gallipoli Peninsula was heavily defended. The Turkish troops fought tenaciously and Allied forces failed to make progress. The operation ended in costly failure, and Churchill became its principal scapegoat.

His meteoric career was over. The Prime Minister, Asquith, sought to create a wartime coalition government, and the Conservatives refused to serve in it unless Churchill were excluded. He hung on to a fragment of office with his appointment in May 1915 as Chancellor of the Duchy of Lancaster – an obscure and ineffectual post. For a man of his energies, inactivity in the midst of a war was unendurable, and he yearned to take an active role in the fighting. He asked the premier for general's rank; instead he was posted, as a major, to the Western Front. After gaining experience with the Grenadier Guards, he went on to command a battalion of the Royal Scots Fusiliers as a lieutenant colonel. He spent seven months at the Front. It was a quiet period in which he saw no significant fighting, though conditions were dangerous. He instilled tremendous spirit into his unit, and livened up the war by ordering frequent barrages fired at the Germans – which brought equally vigorous retaliation. He was an effective officer and won his men's respect and affection, but he was clearly capable of a more important contribution to the war effort. When the amalgamation of two battalions eliminated his post, he left his regiment (shortly to take part in heavy fighting on the Somme) and returned to Parliament.

Earlier in the war Churchill had encouraged research on an armoured vehicle – the 'land cruiser' – which had evolved into the tank. This was first used in battle in 1917, and he was credited with its development. In the same year he was appointed Minister of Munitions and took on the role of supplying the Allied armies with ammunition, an immensely important task that harnessed, once again, his ferocious energy. He fulfilled this function until the war ended in November 1918, and remained in the government as Secretary of State for War. He was therefore responsible for the demobilization of the armed forces, though he was aware that the new era had not brought an end to conflict. The Russian Revolution had been followed by a civil war, and he believed that British troops should be sent to fight the Bolsheviks. The country was, however, in no mood for further strife, and he could not gain enough support for more than limited intervention. It is tempting to wonder how different history would have been if his vision of a crusade against Communism had been realized.

Disembarking from a seaplane after inspecting a flotilla of submarines from the air, Portsmouth, 1914.

His appointment, in October 1911, to the post of First Lord of the Admiralty gave Churchill a field of responsibility for which he was temperamentally well suited. It also gave him the chance to explore the possibilities of new technology and its applications in modern war. He was a passionate supporter of military aviation. As First Lord he found the War Office intent on keeping flying the exclusive preserve of the (Army) Royal Flying Corps, but he fought the Treasury to gain funds and established a Royal Naval Air Service in 1912. Largely equipped with seaplanes, this was based at Eastchurch near Chatham, Kent. Churchill organized it into flights, decided on uniforms and ordered the marking of landing-strips so that they could be seen from the air. 'We are at the Stephenson Age of flying', he remarked (a reference to the early days of steam locomotion). Within 30 years aircraft had, as he predicted, changed out of all recognition.

A flying lesson, Eastchurch, Kent, 1912.

He was so inspired by the Royal Naval Air Service, which he had established, that he took to the skies himself, and found learning to fly the most exhilarating thing he had known since the excitement of campaigning in the Boer War. He took many flying lessons, going up as often as ten times a day. He constantly analysed his mistakes and sought improvement through practice, though his instructors dreaded the responsibility they bore for his life. He did not complete his training, for the pleas of friends and relations eventually led him to abandon what was a highly dangerous pastime.

Churchill takes part in military exercises, Salisbury Plain, 1912.

As a former professional soldier with a love of horses, uniforms and military affairs, it is not surprising that Churchill became an enthusiastic member of a yeomanry (reserve cavalry) regiment – the Queen's Own Oxfordshire Hussars. This unit had always relied heavily on the patronage of the Dukes of Marlborough, and often held its annual camp in the grounds of Blenheim Palace. Churchill's cousin, the 9th Duke, and his brother were members. Churchill attended camps and manoeuvres, and held the rank of major at the time of the outbreak of war in 1914.

With Sir John French, Salisbury Plain, 1912.

Churchill is seen here with Sir John French, who two years later would command the British Expeditionary Force in Europe. Churchill was a close observer of military developments, yet neither he nor anyone else realized that the horse's role in war was effectively finished. Training here for what was expected to be a short war of movement, and in which cavalry would be vital for reconnaissance, these troops could not have imagined the lengthy stalemate, the trenches and the enormous artillery duels that would characterize the conflict once it began.

Visiting the Naval Dockyard with David Lloyd George, Portsmouth, *c.*1912.

Europe was at peace when Churchill became First Lord of the Admiralty in 1911, but his understood purpose was to prepare the Fleet for the war that was considered inevitable. As the Royal Navy expanded, he attended the launch of new vessels as well as inspecting docks, ships, garrisons and training establishments. His energy, inquisitiveness and attention to detail caused some irritation among senior officers but there can be no doubt that he did the job well. Lord Kitchener paid tribute to the fact that, by his order, the Home Fleet had been on a war footing when hostilities broke out in August 1914.

Visiting shipyards, Jarrow, *c.*1912.

Churchill was the most energetic First Lord of the Admiralty in the history of that office. He spent as much as eight months every year away from Whitehall, touring ships and naval establishments. Deeply concerned about the threat from the German Navy, he took a keen interest in the modernization of the Fleet and the technology of new ships.

Attending the launch of the battleship HMS *Iron Duke*, Portsmouth, October 1912.

Churchill had suggested the name of this ship to King George V as a more evocative alternative to the original HMS *Wellington*.

Attending the launch of HMS *Marlborough* – named in honour of his ancestor, October 1912.

It was in fact part of Churchill's job to suggest names for new naval vessels, and he offended King George V twice by proposing to name a ship after the Parliamentarian Oliver Cromwell – a suggestion turned down flat by His Majesty.

With Sir Archibald Sinclair, France, 1916.

The unsuccessful Gallipoli campaign lost Churchill his job as First Lord of the Admiralty and left him with a sense of failure and a need to vindicate himself through action. Posted as an infantry officer to the Western Front, he adopted a practical but eccentric uniform – waterproofs and a French steel helmet – that caused him initially to be suspected of being a spy. This print has been doctored by hand, as was common practice for newpapers, to provide a clean portrait of Churchill for publication. His second-in-command, Sir Archibald Sinclair (later leader of the Liberal Party) would have been cropped out altogether in the final published image.

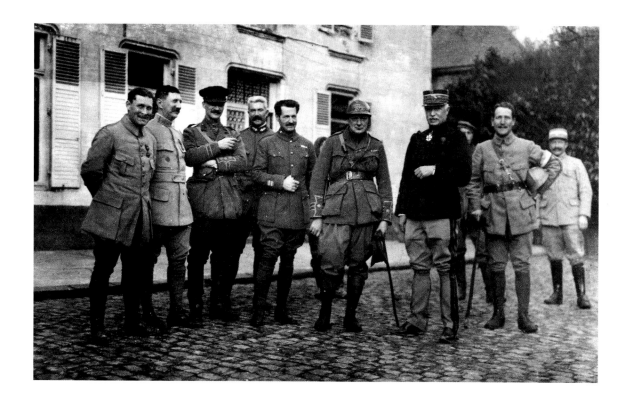

Visiting the headquarters of the French 33rd Division, Ploegsteert, Belgium, 1915.

Though only a major, Churchill's eminent background in British public affairs enabled him to mingle on equal terms with higher-ranking officers.

Despite Churchill having been a professional soldier, his experience was not relevant to the infantry-and-artillery war of the trenches. He was therefore not given command of a brigade, as he had requested, but went to the Front as a major. He spent a month with the Grenadier Guards, whose initial dislike of him as a radical politician gradually melted.

He was then posted, as a lieutenant colonel, to the Royal Scots Fusiliers. This regiment knew little about him, but his charm went to work at once and he became popular. He shared privations, expected no favours, and showed genuine concern for his men. He also pursued a more active prosecution of the war. The artillery barrages he ordered provoked such retaliation that his sector of the Front became too dangerous, and civilians had to be evacuated.

Visiting a munitions factory at Ponder's End, Enfield, London, 1917.

Returning to politics after leaving his regiment, Churchill was appointed Minister for Munitions in July 1917. Having experienced for himself the effects of artillery at the Front, he took an informed interest in the munitions industry, and was able to assure workers of their vital importance to the war effort. The speaker's platform at this factory displays the different calibres of artillery shell produced as well as the American flag – a tribute to Britain's new ally.

Visiting the Beardsmore Armaments Works,
Glasgow, 1918.

Churchill had become convinced that future
battlefields would be dominated by aircraft, artillery
and the 'tank' – a new weapon for which he was
largely responsible. The former cavalry officer believed
that the cavalry horse was now entirely redundant.
'Make catmeat of those foolish animals,' he said.

In the grandstand for a march past, Lille, 1918.

In October 1918 World War I was in its final month. Though none of those in this picture will have known when the end was coming, they were in no doubt that, after years of stalemate, the Allies were now making rapid and extensive advances. Churchill, and a galaxy of staff officers, are watching as Allied troops parade through Lille, which had been liberated after four years of occupation. Behind him, in bowler hat, is his secretary Edward Marsh. His brother Jack (with raised chin) is in the top right corner. Most intriguingly, perhaps, the officer in front of Churchill is Bernard Montgomery, who was to work so closely with him in the next conflict but whom he had not met at this date.

Honouring Transatlantic fliers Alcock and Brown,
London, 1919.

Churchill presents a cheque to the British aviators
John Alcock and Arthur Whitten Brown at a lunch given
in their honour at the House of Lords. They had just
made the first non-stop crossing of the Atlantic by air,
flying a Vickers Vimy aeroplane. As Secretary of State
for Air, Churchill maintained the interest in flying that

he had developed before the war. His Royal Naval
Air Service had merged in 1918 with the Royal Flying
Corps to create the Royal Air Force, but there had been
pressure to disband this service once hostilities ended.
Churchill ensured the RAF's survival and progress.
He was instrumental, for instance, in establishing
the world's first air force officer training college, at
Cranwell in Lincolnshire, in 1920.

Signing of the Treaty of Versailles, Paris, 1919.

World War I ended, in November 1918, with an armistice. Though theoretically a temporary and mutual cessation of hostilities, in practice it was a defeat for the Central Powers, which no longer had the resources to continue the struggle. The peace settlement was drafted at a conference in Paris and handed to the German delegates in June 1919 at the Palace of Versailles. The Treaty was signed in the Hall of Mirrors – a deliberate act of revenge by France, for it was in the same room that the victorious Germans had proclaimed themselves an Empire in 1871.

Germany lost its colonies, navy and air force, while its army was reduced to 100,000 – a shadow of its pre-war strength. Alsace, Lorraine and the rich coalfields of the Saar region were seized. The Rhine became Germany's western frontier, and was 'de-militarized' by the creation of Allied occupation zones. Germany was also obliged to pay war reparations so vast that the cost could only be met by a catastrophic devaluation of its currency.

Delegates at the Cairo Conference, 1921.

A major issue after the war was the fate of vast territories and populations freed from control by the former Central Powers. Becoming Colonial Secretary in 1921, Churchill travelled to Cairo to preside over a conference that created new states out of the ruins of the Ottoman Empire. There were three: Iraq, Transjordan and Palestine. The first two became kingdoms, ruled by Arab chieftains. The third became a British Protectorate. Four years earlier, the Balfour Declaration had committed Britain to supporting a Jewish homeland in Palestine. This led to the Arab-Jewish conflict that has lasted ever since. Churchill relied heavily on the advice of Colonel T. E. Lawrence ('of Arabia') (second row, fourth from right) and the two were to remain friends until Lawrence's death in 1935.

The Churchills attend the wedding of Air Marshal
Sir Hugh Trenchard and the Hon. Mrs Boyle,
London, 1920.

   Trenchard, dubbed the 'father of the air force'
because he had given it much of its character and
established its traditions, had possessed a vision to
match Churchill's own with regard to the future of
air war. The two had been close colleagues and had
fought to gain funding and resources to give the new
service a secure foundation.

   The wedding took place at St Margaret's Church,
Westminster, in which Winston and Clementine had
been married 12 years earlier. Unusually, though
Churchill sports a grey top hat, he is wearing an
ordinary frock coat and is therefore not dressed for
the occasion.

Churchill and his 11-year-old daughter Diana, Hyde Park, 1920.

Though the Great War was over, the King's birthday parade – a major event in the British social and military calendar – was still held under wartime conditions, with the Guardsmen dressed in khaki rather than their familiar scarlet tunics. Churchill attended as Secretary of War, and he was particularly unpopular with the audience. The number of foot guard regiments had recently risen to five with the addition of the Irish and Welsh Guards. Churchill was intent on reducing the number back to three by merging these into the other regiments. As the troops paraded smartly past, many in the crowd cast resentful looks in his direction. In the event, the scheme came to nothing, but he was quoted as grumbling , with reference to the units' cap-badges: 'Star, Thistle and Grenade! They should be the only Guardsmen.'

On the balcony of the House of Commons, Westminster, 1921.

In the aftermath of World War I, Churchill turned his attention to clearing up some of the immense problems it had created. He oversaw the task of demobilizing 2.5 million men from the armed forces, heading off widespread mutiny among discontented troops by adopting a sympathetic policy on the release of servicemen. There was also industrial unrest at home, the question of Ireland, and the prospect of administering vast overseas territories. Most importantly, there was the emergence of Soviet Russia and the West's need to contain this new threat. Churchill's positions as Secretary of State for War (1919–21) and Colonial Secretary (1921–22) involved him deeply in all of these issues. It was a measure of his self-confidence that he enjoyed the challenge of great problems. It was said of him that he never wondered whether he was big enough for a job but whether the job was big enough for him. Here he watches the sovereign's arrival for the State Opening of Parliament.

Arriving in Downing Street for a Cabinet meeting, about to part company with the Liberals and Lloyd George's Coalition Government over the 'Chanak Incident', Westminster, 1922.

Greece went to war because Turkey had refused to cede territory as demanded by the Treaty of Versailles. The UK was involved because British troops were occupying a 'neutral zone' at Chanak on the Dardanelles. Having defeated the Greeks, advancing Turkish troops were in danger of attacking this force. Lloyd George, supported by Churchill, favoured armed resistance to defend the area, but they were in a minority in Cabinet, in government and in the country. A Cabinet split caused the disintegration of Lloyd George's coalition, which the Conservatives had been intent on leaving anyway. In the resulting election Churchill had to fight for votes from his sick-bed as he was stricken with appendicitis. Clementine travelled to Dundee to make speeches for him, but to no avail. He lost badly and this political annihilation evoked his famous remark that he found himself 'without a seat, without a party and without an appendix'. He nevertheless put his leisure to good use by writing *The World Crisis*, his bestselling memoir of the war.

Chapter 4: **AUTHOR AND PROPHET 1922–39**

From the War Office Churchill moved on to become Colonial Secretary, where immense challenges awaited him. Following the end of the war, the Allies were faced with the task of administering and organizing the colonial posses- sions of their former enemies, and in the Middle East there were vast territories that had for centuries been part of the Ottoman Empire. In March 1921 Churchill convened a conference at Cairo to shape the future of the region. This established Palestine and Israel, whose problems have continued ever since, and resulted in the setting up of the Kingdoms of Iraq (whose malleable king ensured the safety of Britain's oil supply) and Transjordan.

Nearer to home there was Ireland, divided by religion, with the six predominantly Protestant northern counties intent on remaining in the UK while the remainder sought to end 800 years of British rule. Churchill advocated harsh military measu- res against the rebels, and only when these failed did he look for a peaceful solution. By a combination of bullying and charm, he won the goodwill of the Irish negotiators, who opted for a treaty as an alternative to anarchy. Separating the Province of Ulster and the Irish Free State – theoretically part of the Empire but in practice independent – the Anglo-Irish Treaty led to civil war between the new government and those who rejected it.

It was at this time that he bought the house – Chartwell, at Westerham in Kent – that was to be his home for the rest of his life. Something of an impulse purchase (Clementine, who was not consulted, always disliked the house) it proved ruinously expensive to convert and maintain, though, with a staff of 18 servants, its owner was clearly not intent on cutting costs. To help finance his home, he published in 1923 the first part of *The World Crisis* – his multi-volume history of World War I (completed 1931). This was his most ambitious work yet, a massive survey of events from his arrival at the Admiralty onwards.

In 1922 Lloyd George's Liberal government had fallen and Churchill was out of office. He was disenchanted with his adopted party, largely because of their soft approach to Socialism, and when he next stood for Parliament, in October 1924, it was as a 'Constitutionalist' – a Conservative in all but name. The following month he entered the Conservative Cabinet as Chancellor of the Exchequer. This appointment delighted him, since he had now equalled his father's achievement. He still possessed Lord Randolph's robe of office (his mother had refused to part with it, saying: 'I am keeping this for my son.').

Despite this heritage, Churchill's tenure of the Chancellorship is not regarded with admiration. His liberal tendencies led him to seek the introduction of widows' pensions and a pruning of military expenditure but, out of his depth in economics, he relied heavily on others' advice. The first of his budgets, in 1925, involved restoring Britain's currency to the Gold Standard. This raised the price of exports and brought down wages. The result was a national crisis – the General Strike – in May 1926.

Churchill's customary response was to treat the Strike as a military campaign. ('We are at war,' he announced.) With the press paralysed, he displayed the same desire to lead from the front that had been seen at Sidney Street. He commandeered Lord Beaverbrook's Fleet Street presses and had a pro-government newspaper – the *British Gazette* – produced by volunteers and naval personnel. The strike ended after less than three weeks and, though he was praised by some for resilience under pressure, the incident bestowed little credit on him.

He remained in government until 1931, when his disagreement with its policy toward India – he was opposed to greater autonomy for the sub-continent – led him to resign. Though he continued as an MP he held no office and entered what were later called his 'wilderness years'. He was widely regarded as a politician whose day was done. He retired to Chartwell and resumed his career as a writer. Without a ministerial salary and in need of funds (he lost heavily in the Wall Street crash) he devoted much of his time to journalism, producing articles on subjects both serious and trivial (which were sometimes penned for him by assistants). He also began a lengthy biography of his ancestor, the first Duke of Marlborough. With a long-standing interest in cinema, he visited Hollywood and suggested that he write the screenplay for a film about his hero, Napoleon, played by his friend Charlie Chaplin. The director Alexander Korda also offered to commission a screenplay about Marlborough.

On a more serious level, he became deeply concerned with the growing menace of Germany. By the mid-1930s – though he had been raising the issue since 1931 – it was clear that this former world power was intent on expunging the shame of defeat. To politicians in Britain, the prospect of another war was unthinkable, and many in government preferred to turn a blind eye to the unwelcome developments in central Europe. The expansion of the German Air Force, for instance – the existence of which was forbidden by the Treaty of Versailles – was ignored lest British objections cause offence in Germany.

Churchill, with no direct influence, could do no more than write on this subject or speak about it in the Commons. Yet though powerless he remained highly influential. He had a number of well-placed allies in different government departments, and these supplied him with sensitive information that fuelled his campaign. But his star had fallen so far that the serious nature of his warnings was dismissed by sections of the press and public as alarmist, exaggerated and bellicose.

The low point of his credibility was March 1938, when the Prime Minister, Neville Chamberlain, returned from Munich with a promise from Hitler that he would annexe no further European territory. Churchill saw the worthlessness of this, but the public believed that the Prime Minister had prevented war, and he was feted as a hero. He had seemingly proved that compromise and negotiation could after all prevent bloodshed.

It was only a matter of months before this notion – and the premier – lost credibility when Hitler seized the rest of Czechoslovakia. Poland was clearly his next victim and the country's security was guaranteed by Britain. When Hitler's troops crossed its border and Britain's protest was ignored, the public could at last see that Churchill had been right.

Churchill arriving at the Savoy Hotel for lunch with David Lloyd George, London, c.1922.

Though he remained the holder of a major Cabinet post and was a towering figure in government, Churchill found himself increasingly out of sympathy with the Liberals. His friendship with Lloyd George, formed during his radical years a decade earlier, continued on a personal level, but the two men had serious professional disagreements. Churchill had sought to crush the nascent menace of Communism by vigorously supporting the White (counter-revolutionary) Russian Army. His obsession with this issue reached the level of fanaticism and caused many to regard him as unbalanced. Lloyd George and other members of his Cabinet realized that a war-weary public would not support yet more fighting, and that there was in fact considerable sympathy among the British working class for the Bolshevist cause. Direct intervention by the British Government in Russian affairs might create serious social unrest at home.

Winston and Clementine at the Derby, Epsom, 1923.

A long-standing member of the Turf Club, Churchill loved racing all his life. Childhood letters to his father contain references to the fortunes of Lord Randolph's horses, and as a young man he once recited, at a dinner party, the names of every Derby winner of the previous 30 years. A regular attender at race meetings, it was only with the wealth acquired from his writings after 1945 that he himself became an owner. He revived Lord Randolph's old racing colours – chocolate and pink – and gave his horses names that sounded as solidly British as he was himself: Colonist and Gibraltar. His interest in the turf increased his popularity with the public, who often backed a horse because it was owned by him.

On the polo field with the Prince of Wales, Worcester Park, 1924.

Churchill had met the Prince of Wales in 1911 when, as Home Secretary, he had been responsible for arranging the young man's investiture as Prince at Caernarvon Castle, and they had an amiable but formal relationship thereafter. At a pivotal moment in the Prince's life – the abdication crisis in 1936 – Churchill was the only major politician who was willing to give him wholehearted support. This flew in the face of public opinion, which strongly condemned the Prince's actions, and suggested to many that Churchill was a bad judge of both character and national mood.

Taking the field for a polo match, Worcester Park, 1924.

Churchill probably first played the game as a cadet at Sandhurst, but his passion for it began when he was posted to India in 1896. His regiment badly wanted to win the inter-Regimental Polo Tournament. They bought a string of well-trained ponies, and practised

unrelentingly. In 1899 they reached the final. Churchill had only recently returned from the Sudan campaign, yet he worked hard enough to get into the team and, in the match, scored three of the goals that helped the 4th Hussars defeat their opponents (the 4th Dragoon Guards) 4–3. He continued to play until he was over 50, often for the House of Commons team.

Dressed for polo, Worcester Park, 1924.

His flair for the game was the more impressive because he played in spite of serious difficulty. As a young officer arriving in India, he had dislocated his right shoulder when trying to land from a boat in rough water. The injury affected him for the rest of his life. He could not lift a polo mallet above the shoulder and could swing it only from the elbow, and so as to prevent a recurrence of the dislocation, he played with his right arm bound to his side. As a cavalry officer he found that the injury also left him unable to swing a sabre. At the Battle of Omdurman in 1898, in which he took part in a cavalry charge, he therefore used a pistol instead. He believed that this saved his life.

Churchill becomes Chancellor of the Exchequer,
London, 1924.

Having parted company with the Liberals, Churchill
was quickly given office when the Conservatives won
the general election in November 1924 – even though
he was not at the time a member of the party. In
his quarter century in politics he had succeeded
in holding high office in both major parties. Some
thought this indicated a principled refusal to follow
political dogma; others saw him as precisely the
opposite – an unprincipled careerist. The Chancellorship was the most senior government post he was to
occupy until he became Prime Minister 16 years later.
His father had served briefly as Chancellor under Lord
Salisbury in the 1880s, and he was delighted to follow
in Lord Randolph's footsteps.

Newly appointed as Chancellor, Churchill leaves
Buckingham Palace with the seals of office, 1924.

Less than a decade earlier, Churchill's ministerial
career had ended – seemingly forever – when he
became the scapegoat for the failed attack on
the Turkish Empire at Gallipoli. Though written

off by his opponents, he had made a remarkable
recovery, gaining three major Cabinet posts in the
intervening years. Now he had achieved the office
that was second only to the premiership; he had good
reason to smile as he returned to his official residence
after seeing the King.

Churchill, campaigning as a 'Constitutionalist', is handed a leaflet from a supporter of his opponent, Westminster, 1924.

He had still been a Liberal when he stood for election in 1923, but the fact that the party enabled Labour to form a government in that year tarred it, in his view, with the socialist brush. He had always been a complicated mix of left and right, but most of his views fitted comfortably with those of his social class and the Conservative Party seemed increasingly to be his natural home. In February 1924 he stood as a candidate for the Abbey Division of Westminster. He was not seeking election as a Conservative – indeed a Conservative candidate stood against him – but the title he gave himself, 'Constitutionalist', meant much the same thing. He campaigned energetically and was almost successful – he lost by only 43 votes. With his usual resilience, he looked for another seat.

Winston S. Churchill

Churchill signs autographs during the general election campaign, Epping, 1924.

When he was a child, both his parents had been famous personalities whose deeds were reported in the press and whose photographs were sold in the shops. From the time he first went away to school, he was asked by fellow pupils to obtain their autographs.

With his unflinching belief in his own destiny, there is little doubt that he expected his own signature to be sought-after one day, and for most of his adult life it was in great demand. He normally gave it cheerfully and willingly, but he asked recipients to donate the sum of one shilling to the Church Army in return. Today it sells for many thousands of times that amount.

Churchill addressing local workers prior to the
general election, Woodford, 1924.

Though his previous seats had been in Scotland or
the north of England, Churchill was to be associated
with Essex for the majority of his parliamentary career.
Though his background was far removed from that of

men like these, his long practice in electioneering
had made him skilled at tailoring his remarks to suit
his listeners, and his natural wit usually impressed
some voters. With his fear of Bolshevism, which
was particularly virulent at this time, he regarded
the working class with a great deal of suspicion.

Churchill speaks to voters in an Essex constituency, Waltham Abbey, 1924.

Though he looks benign, and has obviously amused his listeners, local Conservatives would have had serious doubts about his candidature. He was a renegade whose desertion to the Liberals exactly two decades earlier had not been forgiven, and it was not quite clear which party he was now aligned with. Fortunately for him, the post-war political world was going through a period of readjustment and renewal. Old loyalties and alliances were breaking down, and in this fluid atmosphere he was elected. Shortly after this election, he once again became a Conservative, bringing his political odyssey full circle.

Arriving at Westminster Abbey for the funeral
of Lord Rosebery, Westminster, 1925.

Churchill had a genuine admiration for Rosebery,
who had been Prime Minister at a time when he
himself had been a young army officer. Rosebery
had set out in life with three ambitions – to marry
both beauty and wealth; to become Prime Minister,
and for one of his horses to win the Derby. He had
succeeded in all three. Churchill was impressed by
men who – as he had done himself – had started by
making outrageous demands on life and had pursued
their desires with consistency and determination.

Churchill campaigning, Woodford, 1924.

Even after long years of speech-making, Churchill took considerable care over his public appearances. Speaking without a microphone, and often without notes, he used his exceptional memory to retain the statistics and other information he would need. Basing his oratory partly on the style of Gibbon and Macaulay – authors who had greatly influenced him in his youth – as well as on his father's speeches, Churchill in fact owed most of his education as a speaker and parliamentarian to Bourke Cockran, an Irish-American lawyer and politician who was a friend of Lady Randolph. Cockran, said to have been the greatest orator and conversationalist of his generation in the United States, recognized the potential of the young Churchill and for a time acted as his mentor.

Churchill and his police bodyguard arrive at
10 Downing Street, London, 1926.

As a consistently unpopular politician, Churchill
was often in need of protection. His family had been
shadowed by a police detective during the suffragette
era, when threats had been made to kidnap his
children. As one of the prime movers behind the
Anglo-Irish Treaty (as Colonial Secretary he became
responsible for its implementation), he was targeted
by Irish Republicans. He possessed, however, immense
personal courage and was genuinely unafraid of
danger. At this period he carried a personal weapon
– a Colt revolver – and told his bodyguard, who had
warned him of suspicious men lurking at a roadside:
'If they want trouble they can have it.' With the onset
of the General Strike, he faced danger once again.

Churchill makes his way into Parliament through a supportive crowd during the General Strike, Whitehall, 1926.

Churchill's policy of returning Britain's currency to the Gold Standard was blamed for forcing down wages, and this caused a major strike that lasted almost three weeks in May 1926. The government did not flinch in its resistence to this action, and gained the approval of many middle class voters. Churchill's contribution to fighting the strikers was to organize the publication of an uncompromisingly worded newspaper, the *British Gazette*, and oversee its distribution. Though hated by radicals, he was respected by many of those who either did not support the strike or merely found the resulting chaos irksome. Such people were clearly in evidence here as he entered Palace Yard, followed by his Parliamentary Private Secretary, Robert Boothby.

Churchill receives an honorary degree, Bristol
University, 1925.

Until he started to make headway as a statesman,
Churchill was self-conscious about his lack of a
university education. By the time he began to receive
honorary degrees, at Bristol and Oxford in the 1920s,
the public was aware of his gifts and accomplishments.

Carried aloft by students as Churchill is elected
Chancellor, Bristol University, 1929.

The Chancellorship of a great university was a
recognition of ability that the self-educated Churchill
greatly appreciated – even though in this instance it
involved a good-natured manhandling by the under-
graduates, who mock-arrested him and carried
him down the steps. At subsequent university
ceremonies he wore Chancellor's robes and had a
page in a three-cornered hat to carry his train. He
enjoyed academic ceremonial as much as formal
civic, parliamentary and military occasions.

Churchill leaves 11 Downing Street,
Whitehall, 1929.

Though not a great Chancellor of the Exchequer,
he remained in the post long enough to present five
consecutive budgets, a rare achievement, last attained
by William Gladstone. He found economics ('those
damned dots') difficult to understand, though he
had his famous power of concentration as well as
the help of able assistants. He yearned for the days
when his government duties had been military and he
was on surer ground, remarking of his departmental
colleagues: 'I wish they were admirals or generals. I
speak their language. But after a while these fellows
start talking Persian. And then I am sunk.'

The Churchill family walks to the House of
Commons on budget day, Whitehall, 1929.
    Churchill carries the budget proposals in a dispatch
box. As is British custom, the box itself is the subject
of great curiosity as press and public speculate about
its mysterious contents, and the presence of family
members and grinning passers-by gives the occasion

something of a carnival atmosphere. Visible in
the picture are Churchill's daughter Sarah and his
Parliamentary Private Secretary, Robert Boothby
(Clementine, and their son Randolph were also there).
They are accompanied by a plain-clothes police officer
in addition to the uniformed 'bobby' in front, though
by present-day standards this security was negligible.

Tending the fish pond, Chartwell, c.1930.

For a man who was so preoccupied with work and important issues of state, Churchill had a remarkably full and varied private life. Though he could be extremely tough in political argument, and could be sanguine about the sight of the dead on battlefields, he had an extremely tender side, which caused him to befriend animals. He claimed a natural empathy with pigs and was especially fond of butterflies, cats and ornamental fish. He is seen here looking at his pet carp. Twenty years later, after World War II, someone killed all his fish by throwing a hand-grenade into their pond – proof that even after his role in saving Europe from Nazi domination, he continued to provoke dislike.

Churchill as artist, Chartwell, c.1930.

The hobby for which he became best known was painting. He began during World War I when out of office, and received tutoring from the Irish painter John Lavery and his wife. For the rest of his life, his canvases gave him release from the storms of war and politics. He once said that: 'If it wasn't for painting I couldn't live. I couldn't bear the strain of things.' His paintings were regarded highly enough to earn him election as an honorary member of the Royal Academy, and he once had a one-man show in Paris under the pseudonym 'Charles Maurin'. His pictures – mostly landscapes, and with few figures in them – are still treasured by the individuals or galleries that own them.

Churchill building a wall on his estate,
Chartwell, *c*.1930.

Yet another accomplishment was his ability to lay
bricks, an unlikely occupation for a duke's grandson,
but one that he found both creative and therapeutic.
After appropriate instruction, he began to build walls
in the garden of his home. They still stand, a testimony
to the skill he acquired. In playful spirit, he joined
the Amalgamated Union of Building Trade Workers,
paying the five-shilling fee and receiving a union card,
but members of the union, for whom he was a major
antagonist after his handling of the General Strike,
were angered that his application had been accepted
and sent the money back.

Churchill's country home, Chartwell, *c.*1939.

He fell in love with this rather ugly house at first sight in 1922 and bought it without consulting Clementine. Situated near Westerham in west Kent, 25 miles (40km) from London, it was convenient for Parliament as well as for the numerous visitors who came down from London. Financially, the house was a disaster. Once bought, with the proceeds of a legacy, it cost an immense sum to renovate, and proved so expensive to maintain that the Churchills thought of renting it out or selling it. After World War II, a group of his friends and admirers bought it to preserve as a memorial, enabling the Churchills to occupy it for their lifetimes. It is now owned by the National Trust.

Einstein visits, Chartwell, *c.*1933.

Churchill's prestige ensured that his home was visited by a large number of people eminent in politics, finance, the arts and academia, both from Britain and elsewhere. He was usually a gracious host, and was at his best amid the stimulation of great minds and good talk. Albert Einstein, whose discoveries would lead to the development of the atomic bomb a few years after this visit, would have found him superficially well-informed on scientific matters, full of questions and eager to increase his understanding. Some guests, however, found the consumption of alcohol, the late nights and the atmosphere of endless debate at the Chartwell dinner table rather overwhelming. It was reported that Churchill once shouted at his ebullient son: 'Don't interrupt me while I'm interrupting!'

Charlie Chaplin comes to tea, Chartwell, 1931.

Churchill was a lifelong fan of the cinema, and was not highbrow – he revelled in slapstick comedy and cheap melodrama, and might see a favourite film many times over. He met Chaplin on several occasions, most notably in Hollywood while he was making a lecture-tour of the United States in 1929. In spite of the fact that the two men disagreed passionately about politics, they established a warm personal friendship. Churchill greatly admired Chaplin's ability as an actor and mimic, and was very keen to collaborate with him on a film script. Chaplin twice visited Chartwell.

Churchill addresses French politicians, Paris, 1936.

Throughout the 1930s Churchill was preoccupied with two major issues – his opposition to greater self-determination for India, and his concern with Germany's reawakening power. He became a frequent speaker on the latter subject in the House of Commons, and also wrote about it in the press.

This made him a thorn in the side of the British Government and the Foreign Office, both of whom were avoiding comment for fear of offending Hitler. His stand gained him a small following in Parliament and a reputation that travelled abroad – Hitler and Goebbels were infuriated by any notion of Churchill returning to government. In France, he addressed politicians. As

a lifelong Francophile – though a rather idiosyncratic French speaker – Churchill was at home in France. As his concern mounted over German rearmament, he realized how much Europe needed a strong French state as a counterweight. He hoped that the country's large army would be led by resolute politicians when the crisis came.

Churchill and his shadow, Whitehall, c.1939.

Brendan Bracken, a mysterious, self-made financier and politician of Irish origin, arrived at Chartwell one day in 1924 and went on to become Churchill's friend and champion, having entered Parliament in 1929. As an MP he provided, with Anthony Eden, the core of a group that supported Churchill in his campaign to raise awareness of the German threat. Churchill's sense of urgency increased after 1935, when the Anglo-German Naval Agreement allowed Hitler to disregard the restrictions placed on his country's navy at the end of World War I by the Treaty of Versailles. Though out of office and out of government, Churchill had access to accurate, restricted information and in debate he could brandish statistics like weapons in his fight against timidity and inertia. He was supplied with this data, surreptitiously, by sympathizers such as Desmond Morton, the head of the Industrial Intelligence Centre, and Wing Commander Torr Anderson, who kept him apprised of the expansion of Germany's Air Force, which was undertaken in secret.

Churchill the author, Chartwell, 1939.

Out of high political office, Churchill spent a good deal of the 1930s on two of his great literary projects: his biography of the First Duke of Marlborough and the extensive *History of the English-Speaking Peoples*, which he had to abandon until after the war. Though highly regarded as an author, his historical works are frankly too lengthy for the general reader and too subjective to be of value to impartial scholars. He did not write in a conventional manner: rather he hired a team of researchers, assistants and secretaries. They assembled and edited the material; he read it, formed his opinions and then dictated the narrative to secretaries, who often worked in relays to accommodate his energy and unusual working hours.

Winston is back! Churchill rejoins the Cabinet, Whitehall, 1939.

After years of watching the rearmament of Germany and the dithering of his own government, Churchill was at last in a position to fulfil a useful function. He became First Lord of the Admiralty but, as the most forceful and – in military terms – experienced member of the Cabinet, he became in effect the nation's war leader. Unlike the men around him – the 'Old Gang' – he was not associated in the public mind with the now discredited policy of appeasement. Seen here, in November 1939, are, back row: Sir Kingsley Wood (Secretary of State for Air), Churchill (First Lord of the Admiralty), Leslie Hore-Belisha (Secretary of State for War), Lord Hankey (Minister without Portfolio). Front row: Lord Halifax (Foreign Secretary), Sir John Simon (Chancellor of the Exchequer), Neville Chamberlain (Prime Minister), Sir Samuel Hoare (Lord Privy Seal), Lord Chatfield (Minister for Coordination of Defence). Once appointed Prime Minister, Churchill was also to assume the role of Minister of Defence.

Chapter 5: **STERNER DAYS 1939–45**

The outbreak of war brought Churchill back into government. He was appointed First Lord of the Admiralty and, for the second time, presided over the Royal Navy through the opening phase of a world conflict. The Fleet was sent a signal: 'Winston is back!'. They had a comfortable relationship.

He may have been subordinate to Chamberlain, but in practice the premier was completely overshadowed by the First Lord. Churchill was not only a stronger, more charismatic and more inspiring personality, he also had far greater moral authority. Having been out of power during the period of appeasement, he was untarnished by its image of gullibility and failure. Already the country's de facto war leader, he seemed to many the obvious premier for this new and dangerous era.

The war began with a winter of inactivity – the 'Phoney War' – and only in the spring of 1940 did the tempo increase. In April, Hitler invaded Denmark and Norway (vital to the supply of iron ore), and a British expedition to secure the port of Narvik was a costly failure. Churchill, its instigator, escaped blame because he had at least taken positive action against the enemy. Chamberlain lost so much credibility that his resignation was demanded in the Commons. He departed office on 9 May. The next morning, German troops invaded Western Europe.

On that day Churchill became Prime Minister. Though not the most popular or stable candidate among those in power (the King would have preferred Lord Halifax, who declined) he was the only senior politician who seemed to have a clear vision, backed by iron determination. He himself later recalled: 'I felt as if I were walking with destiny, and that all my past life had been but a preparation for this hour and for this trial.' It was beyond question that his 40 years of public service, in peace and war, had equipped him with qualities of experience and temperament that were uniquely suited to the task ahead.

In the weeks that followed, France capitulated and British troops only just escaped from Dunkirk. Churchill's response was to speak. His addresses to the Commons, broadcast to the public on the BBC, magnificently caught the mood of a nation that knew it was in for a long ordeal but was intent on defiance. His key phrases – 'blood, toil, tears and sweat', 'finest hour', 'fight them on the beaches' – have lost none of their impact for having been so often repeated. Churchill was making clear that Britain must stand up to the seemingly invincible Hitler, not only for its own security and independence but for the dignity and freedom of all mankind. Those who lived in that time and place had been handed by fate an unprecedented and terrifying challenge. For the sake of history and of future generations they must accept it, though it would bring terrible hardship.

And this was not long in coming. Hitler decided to invade Britain during August 1940. Before his ships could sail, the RAF must be destroyed. The German Luftwaffe set out to do this through a series of unrelenting raids. They almost succeeded, but owing to advanced radar and the resourcefulness of their opponents they could not gain air superiority. Without this, the invasion stalled. Having failed to defeat the RAF, the Luftwaffe turned on British cities, and launched a massive bombing campaign – the Blitz. This strengthened resolve to fight on and, on his many visits to bombed areas, Churchill was often greeted with shouts of: 'Give it 'em back, Winnie!' The Blitz lasted into 1941 but this, too, was a failure (both British morale and industrial production survived). Hitler had, in any case, lost interest. Planning to invade Russia, he believed that Britain had been knocked out of the war and could not recover.

It was vital that the Empire be protected. This meant securing the Suez Canal and the route to India. The war, lost in Europe, therefore moved to the Mediterranean and North Africa. Here too, matters went badly for Britain at the beginning. Rommel, the German commander, bested several of his Allied counterparts; it was only in the autumn of 1942 that he met his match in Montgomery – and was defeated at El Alamein.

By that time the nature of the war had entirely changed. Hitler's invasion of the USSR in June 1941 had turned this immensely powerful country from ally to enemy. After spectacular initial successes, German forces gradually became mired in its vast expanses, and no matter how many Russians they killed or captured, the country's seemingly unlimited pool of manpower could provide more. German losses were immense.

In December of that year, Japan had made a bid to dominate East Asia by destroying the US Pacific Fleet at Pearl Harbor. Churchill's will to win had already impressed President Roosevelt, who had allowed US war *matériel* to be lent to Britain. Now Hitler – supporting his Japanese ally – declared war on the USA, which became a full-fledged ally of Britain.

Out of these circumstances was created the partnership – the 'Big Three' – that won the war and shaped the future of Europe. The three leaders were entirely different in character, but all were realists who understood that they could only defeat Hitler by working together. Churchill formed a personal friendship, and an extremely effective working relationship, with Roosevelt. Against all expectations, the aristocratic Churchill also succeeded in winning Stalin's respect. Since the Russian leader would not travel to the West, Churchill was obliged to make several arduous journeys to see him in Russia. There he had the difficult task of resisting demands for a 'second front' in the West to take pressure off Russia. This had to wait until Anglo-American forces were sufficiently built up.

By 1944, Germany had clearly lost the war. That summer, the Allies obliged Stalin by invading France. A massive Allied aerial bombardment was reducing German cities to rubble. In the East, Russian victories at Stalingrad and Kharkov had turned the tide. By this stage, Churchill was only an honorary member of the Big Three. America and Russia – which commanded the major resources – now ran the war, and it was largely the force of his personality that kept Britain at the 'top table'. Nevertheless, he was now a man of unassailable international stature. After the European war ended, in May 1945, he was obliged to dissolve his wartime coalition and face a general election. His success in this seemed to many a foregone conclusion.

The Prime Minister, Whitehall, 1940.

Though a strong contender for the premiership in 1940, Churchill was not the favoured candidate. The thoughtful and dignified Foreign Secretary, Lord Halifax, seemed a more stable leader for the testing time to come than the mercurial Churchill. However, Halifax knew that he lacked the necessary qualities and that as a peer he could not lead the government in the Commons. Churchill realized his dream of becoming Prime Minister at the most perilous moment in modern British history. That day, German forces invaded Western Europe. 'I hope that it is not too late', he said, 'I am very much afraid it is'. In fact, he was the right man to lead Britain in this dire situation. Despite his private concern, he radiated a determination and confidence that inspired the nation. The photograph above, taken in the Cabinet Room at 10 Downing Street, captures this aspect of his leadership. The firm jaw, unflinching gaze and stubborn, bulldog features – familiar through press and posters – had already made him a national icon.

The Prime Minister signs an Anglo-Polish agreement, Whitehall, 1940.

Churchill's predecessor as Prime Minister, Neville Chamberlain, had guaranteed to go to war against Germany if Poland was attacked. Hitler had ordered the invasion of the country a few months later. Thousands of Polish servicemen escaped and made their way to Britain, where they formed Army, Navy and Air Force units that made a disproportionate contribution to the Allied effort. A Polish government-in-exile was also established in London. Churchill admired the fighting qualities of this martial people, and later in the war was to remark that, when the Allies wanted to deal especially harshly with enemy resistance, 'we send in the Poles.' They fought valiantly and well at Cassino and Arnhem.

Inspecting emergency nursing staff, London, 1940.

It had been expected for years that another European war would involve fierce air raids and very heavy civilian casualties. Britain had been preparing for such a situation since 1938, when the outbreak of hostilities first seemed imminent. In the event it was not until almost a year after the war began that the bombing of cities commenced. The destruction proved as terrible as had been feared, but the emergency services coped, and showed considerable bravery. These young women, from a unit of the St John's Ambulance Brigade, were part of that heroic effort.

Returning by boat from an inspection of bomb
damage in the docks, London, 1940.

Churchill and Clementine made frequent visits
to stricken areas, and both showed a degree of
personal courage in doing so – for raids might still
be in progress when they arrived. The presence of
the Prime Minister at these scenes made him highly
popular. He might be greeted as 'Good Old Winnie',
and his openly tearful reaction to scenes of
destruction gave the clear impression that he
cared about the victims. Clementine adopted
during the war a headscarf of the kind worn by
female factory workers. This was a gesture of
solidarity, suggesting that all classes were united
in the effort to win the war. Her husband's famous
siren suit gave the same impression.

The Prime Minister visits rescue workers,
Ramsgate, 1941.

Churchill's trademarks – his walking stick and cigar
– were greatly enjoyed by the public when he toured
afflicted areas. Though never without these personal
talismans he was obliged, like any citizen, to obey
regulations by carrying a gas mask and steel helmet,
and to wear the latter when appropriate. The helmet
increased his look of pugnacity, but though it looked
perfectly ordinary, it was lined inside with a velvet
band made for him by Lock & Co., the prestigious
St James's Street hatters.

Winston boosts morale, London, 1940.

 Visiting a crowded street (the smiling faces and undamaged buildings suggest that this is not a bombed district), Churchill is mobbed by members of the public while police try to keep them back. Though pictures often suggest that he was alone, he always travelled with an entourage that included local officials as well as secretaries, assistants and senior officers.

The House of Commons receives a direct hit, Westminster, 1941.

On 11 May 1941 the Houses of Parliament suffered severe damage in an air raid. The Prime Minister, accompanied by Brendan Bracken, visited the smoking ruins the following day. The sight, perhaps predictably, brought Churchill to tears, but it increased the determination of the British people to win. Parliament moved to Church House, a large building nearby, and carried on with its business. When plans were made for the rebuilding of the Commons it was suggested to Churchill that the traditional shape of the House – two banks of seats divided by an aisle in the style of a church – should be abandoned in favour of a semi-circular forum like the American Congress. He strongly objected. He felt that the traditional layout, in which Members debated face to face, had served Britain well. It was retained.

Viewing more devastation, London, c.1941.

Churchill was greatly impressed by the British people's resilience under the continuing aerial bombardment. His own home – 10 Downing Street – was damaged in air raids, but night after night he refused to descend into his bunker beneath Whitehall, preferring to watch proceedings from the rooftop. One night while viewing a raid he seated himself comfortably on a chimney. Those in the bunker below were almost asphyxiated until someone traced the source of the problem, and asked the Prime Minister to stand up.

Churchill with a Tommy gun, England, c.1941.

As an old soldier, the Prime Minister was curious about the equipment used by British troops. While inspecting a unit he examined a Thompson sub-machine gun. This weapon, manufactured for the US Army and fitted here with a drum magazine, was associated in the public mind – via the cinema – with American gangsters. Churchill's hat, suit and cigar made him look so much the part that Nazi propaganda seized on the image and, painting out everyone else in the scene, put it on posters that touted him as an arch-criminal.

Testing a Sten gun, England, c.1941.

This time the Prime Minister aims a Sten gun, a
British-manufactured sub-machine gun that was so
simple to assemble that each weapon cost only four
shillings and sixpence. However, they were liable to
jam when fired, and were not popular with troops.
The man to the right of Churchill is his police bodyguard Inspector Walter Thompson.

Inspecting British armour, England, 1941.

The Prime Minister is pictured here, on a tour of inspection, about to take the salute of the Eastern Command Armoured Division. As one of those chiefly responsible for developing the tank during the previous war, he had a special interest in these vehicles, and indeed one member of the species was named after him (an honour he shared with Oliver Cromwell). He said about this, 'It was ordered off the drawing board, and large numbers went into production very quickly. As might be expected, it had many defects and teething troubles, and when these became apparent the tank was appropriately christened the "Churchill".'

Visiting coastal defences, Scotland, 1940.

The summer of 1940 was largely given over to preparing defences against the expected German invasion. Beaches were declared out of bounds to civilians and were heavily guarded. Pill boxes and barbed wire appeared along vulnerable stretches of the coastline, road signs were removed to confuse paratroops and fields were littered with cars and other objects to prevent aircraft landing. The Polish Army was assigned to protect the east coast of Scotland, and this photograph shows Churchill and senior officers visiting them. The commander of the Polish forces, General Sikorski, is just visible to the left of the tank.

Churchill says farewell to the President, Newfoundland, 1941.

Britain's only hope of survival was to engage the United States in the war against Hitler, and Churchill made vigorous efforts to do this by wooing the country's President, Franklin Roosevelt. He arranged a meeting at Placentia Bay off Newfoundland in March 1941. Both men arrived in warships, aboard which their discussions took place. Churchill's case was greatly helped by the fact that Roosevelt already believed America must join in the war. Nevertheless, on this occasion the two men formed a sound working relationship that was to be cemented by many other meetings. In this photograph Churchill waves to the President's ship, the USS *Augusta*, as it departs. They would meet again that December.

The warlord at sea, England, 1941.

Churchill's V-for-victory sign became his most famous trademark. It was in fact borrowed from occupied Europe, where it stood for *victoire* in France or *vrijheid* (freedom) in Flemish. He used it indiscriminately, presenting the front and – as here – the back of the hand, which caused some confusion, for in Britain the latter is considered extremely rude. The gesture spread from Churchill throughout the Allied armies and the whole world.

Prime Minister Churchill begins a warm and
vital partnership with President Roosevelt,
Newfoundland, 1941.

Roosevelt, who had been crippled by polio, had to be
supported as he came aboard HMS *Prince of Wales* by
his son, Elliott, who wears the uniform of a captain in
the US Marine Corps. To mark this meeting in Placentia
Bay, Roosevelt provided for each member of the British
battleship's crew a present of food and cigarettes – a
charming gesture that was greatly appreciated by men
used to rationing and hardship. The result of the
meeting was a jointly issued 'Atlantic Charter' affirming
the principles of democracy, though America was not
yet ready to join the war to defend them.

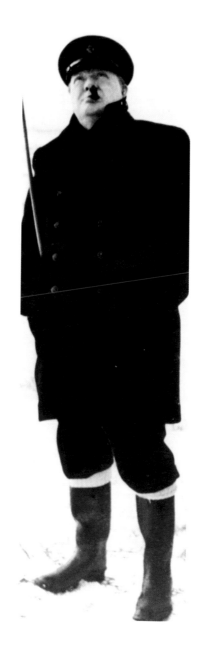

Churchill in naval rig, Newfoundland, 1941.

Always given to dressing up, Churchill loved to wear uniforms. As First Lord of the Admiralty he had become a member of the Royal Yacht Squadron, the most exclusive British sailing club. When travelling by sea, he wore the Squadron's blue, brass-buttoned reefer jacket and peaked cap. In this picture he has also, unusually, adopted sea-boots.. Not everyone found this impressive. 'Looks like a ruddy park-keeper,' was the comment of one sailor as he stood in line waiting to be inspected, and some naval personnel considered his costume flippant.

A story was told that during the Atlantic meeting, an American warship was attempting to tie up alongside HMS *Prince of Wales*. An American Chief Petty Officer noticed a sailor on the afterdeck of the British vessel and shouted 'Ahoy, bear a hand and secure this line!' The man did so, and turned out to be Churchill.

Churchill, a tireless traveller, visits the scene
of bitterest fighting, Western Desert, 1942.

When the war moved to the immense spaces of the
North African desert, Churchill went to see the area for
himself. He also sought to add, by his presence, some
impetus to the Allied effort (only a few months later,
Montgomery would defeat Rommel at El Alamein). He
loved to visit the scenes of action and, to his wife's
frequent dismay, disregarded the risks involved in
wartime travel as well as the danger once he arrived.

Churchill with the troops, Western Desert, 1942.

For a man in his 60s to travel so frequently between countries, continents and theatres of war, even in the relative comfort he often enjoyed, was remarkable. That he could get through a punishing schedule of meetings, conferences, visits and inspections was a tribute to his mental and physical toughness. His health in fact suffered seriously: he had a heart attack while at the White House early in 1942 (nothing was known about this until long afterwards), and the following year he caught pneumonia.

By the time he made this visit to the North African desert in August 1942, the siren suit he is wearing here was world-famous. Inspired by the overalls he had worn when bricklaying at Chartwell, it consisted of a single garment, zipped up the front, made from velvet or worsted. It could be put on in a matter of seconds if he needed to dress in a hurry. Though they looked informal and even slovenly, the suits were made by Turnbull & Asser, the exclusive gentlemen's outfitter in London's Jermyn Street. They did not start a craze and nobody else was ever seen wearing a siren suit, although Churchill gave one to the King as a Christmas present in 1940.

Churchill meets Eisenhower, North Africa, 1943.

Once America had entered the war, US troops began to arrive in the desert to add their weight to Commonwealth forces. Eisenhower was not an officer with extensive combat experience – he had spent many years coaching army sports teams – yet his equable temperament and pleasant personality made him an effective co-ordinator and commander. After involvement in Operation Husky, the Allied invasion of Italy from North Africa, Eisenhower prepared for an even bigger challenge – overall command of the D-Day landings. The two men would meet often – Eisenhower would be President during Churchill's second term as Prime Minister in the 1950s.

Visiting troops, Western Desert, 1942.

The desert war had produced no clear victor, though the Allies were getting the worst of it. In the summer of 1942, driven eastwards as far as Egypt, they fortified a defence-line based on El Alamein, and stopped the German advance there. The two sides dug in, the Germans failed to break through and, in October, the Allies drove them back in a fierce counter-attack. Montgomery, a diligent and painstaking commander, slowly built up manpower and weaponry until he was able to deal effectively with the enemy. His victory was decisive, saved Egypt and forced the Afrika Korps to retreat towards Libya, though Montgomery was criticized for a slow pursuit that left German forces intact.

An uncharacteristic wartime moment as Churchill
nurses the baby son of Sir Miles Lampson, the
British Resident in Egypt, c.1942.

Visiting the African theatre of war, Churchill sits
in the garden of the British Ambassador's residence
in Cairo with Victor, the son of the Ambassador. He
was not, himself, a natural parent – he was too
egotistical and preoccupied – yet all his own children
were devoted to him because of his sense of fun.
Many other children liked him, either because he
treated them like adults or for the opposite reason
– that he had no difficulty in reverting to their level.
While he was in disgrace after the Gallipoli fiasco
in 1915, his nephew describes him performing a
magnificent gorilla impression up a tree, with a
typical lack of self-consciousness.

The kindly uncle, Egypt, c.1942.

Churchill could be indulgent of small children when he noticed them. Now becoming elderly, he had developed the bald and cherubic appearance that enabled him to quip: 'All babies look like me.'

Once the initial phase of the war – the threat of German invasion and the Blitz – was over, the Prime Minister's life became increasingly taken up with what would today be called 'shuttle diplomacy'. He flew or sailed – accompanied by a sizeable retinue of officers, advisers, secretaries and assistants – to several different parts of the world, to meet with leaders and military commanders and to plan the prosecution of the war. In North Africa his informal clothing became notoriously eccentric. He wore suits and topees, a siren suit, slippers and stetsons (as here). After a bout of pneumonia in 1943 he began to be seen in a green silk dressing gown covered in a design of gold dragons, and would walk about all day in this, the cord trailing behind him.

With Jan Smuts, Egypt, *c.*1942.

One great pleasure for Churchill was the fact that so many of the leaders with whom he dealt were, or became, personal friends. To some extent it seemed as if the world was run by a small coterie comprising Churchill and his acquaintances.

Roosevelt once wrote to him: 'It is fun to share this decade with you'.

He had first met Jan Smuts in 1899 when he was captured during the South African War. Smuts, a Cambridge-educated lawyer, had been the Boer officer who had decided that he should be imprisoned as a

soldier and not released as a journalist. In spite of this they later enjoyed a personal friendship and a good working relationship. Smuts, who became a field marshal as well as South African Prime Minister, steered his country into the war on the Allied side despite an element of Boer sympathy for the Nazis.

Coming to terms with the French, Casablanca, 1943.

One statesman with whom Churchill did not have a happy relationship was the Free French leader, Charles de Gaulle, who struck him as arrogant and ungrateful for the shelter and facilities that Britain had given him. While Churchill recognized de Gaulle's ability and potential, Roosevelt hated him. Also present at this meeting was General Giraud (far left), the French Commissioner for North Africa. The two men saw themselves as the personification of 'Fighting France' and were serious rivals, as their body language perhaps indicates. It was at this conference that the policy of unconditional surrender was settled – only complete capitulation, rather than a negotiated end to the war – would be tolerated by the Allies.

The first great wartime conference, Quebec, 1943.

In August Churchill sailed to Quebec for another meeting with Roosevelt. He is seen here being officially welcomed by the Canadian Prime Minister, William Lyon McKenzie King. Though the British premier's travels were undertaken for the most serious of purposes, there is no doubt that he enjoyed the escape from wartime Britain and the stimulation of other lands – particularly the bustling nations of North America.

Churchill aboard HMS *Prince of Wales*,
England, 1941.

Coming on board the ship that would take him to
meet President Roosevelt, the Prime Minister displays
his love of cats. This animal would have been more
than a mere pet – cats were vital for pest control
aboard ships. Tragically, a few months after the voyage
to Newfoundland, HMS *Prince of Wales*, like its sister-
ship HMS *Repulse*, was sunk by the Japanese off the
coast of Malaya, with the loss of much of her crew.

Churchill on his way to visit Niagara Falls, c.1943.

While in Canada for the Quebec Conference, Churchill went by train to visit Niagara Falls with his daughter
Mary. She is seen here in the uniform of the Auxiliary
Territorial Service, a women's army unit. Also with him
is his Scotland Yard bodyguard, Inspector Thompson.

When travelling, Churchill had always had the
ability to combine a punishing work schedule with the
normal pleasures of sightseeing. His concentration on
important affairs was balanced by a curiosity to visit
well-known places. Here he is standing outside the
rear door of a railroad observation car. These vehicles

were much utilized by politicians in North America.
The railed-off area of the viewing platform was ideally
suited to campaigning, for it raised the candidate
above the heads of the crowd and provided an ideal
stage for speeches. In this instance, it gave Canadians
a chance to see the legendary British premier.

Churchill with Allied leaders including Canadian
Premier, Mackenzie King (left), General Eisenhower
(centre) and the South African Prime Minister, Jan
Smuts (right), Quebec, 1943.

As a result of the discussions at Quebec, the
Allies adopted – though they were later to abandon
it – the Morganthau Plan. This sought to both punish
and safeguard Germany after an Allied victory,
by dismantling its industry and reducing the
country to a pastoral economy. Hitler saw the
proposals and described them as a national
'death sentence.' They helped stiffen German
determination not to surrender when the war
was clearly lost in 1945.

Churchill and Roosevelt with Stalin, Tehran, 1943.

The 'Big Three' met for the first time in December, though Churchill had visited Stalin in Moscow the previous year and assessed his character. The post-war dismemberment of Germany was discussed, and it became obvious to the two Western leaders that Stalin intended to occupy Poland and much of Eastern Europe after the war. Relations had improved since 1942, when Stalin had demanded the opening of an Allied 'second front' to ease the pressure on his own troops. This had been impossible, but he had been persuaded to accept Allied efforts in North Africa as evidence of their commitment to victory.

The Stalingrad Sword, Tehran, 1943.

When Churchill attended the conference with Roosevelt and Stalin in Tehran in November 1943, the Prime Minister brought a symbolic gift for their Russian allies. The Stalingrad Sword was a beautifully crafted weapon made, by the firm of Wilkinson, from steel, silver and rock crystal, its handle covered in gold wire. Its design – that of a medieval sword – was chosen by the King, and it bore the inscription: 'To the steel-hearted citizens of Stalingrad, the gift of King George the Sixth, in token of the homage of the British people.' The sword was presented to Stalin by Churchill in the presence of an Anglo-Russian guard of honour. The Battle of Stalingrad had ended ten months earlier, and its significance in changing the course of the war was appreciated by all the Allies.

The sword was made partly by an RAF corporal, L.G. Durbin, who was in peacetime a sword crafts-man and who gained leave for the task. Three more versions were created, of which one is displayed in Wilkinson Sword's museum in London.

The last conference of Allied leaders held during the war, Yalta, 1945.

Yalta was a resort on the Black Sea. The participants were photographed in the Livadia Palace, the former summer home of Tsar Nicholas II. By this stage in the war, America and Russia were running the conflict. The size of their armies and industrial plants ensured the defeat of Hitler and showed that the world was already dominated by these two superpowers. At Yalta the Western Allies agreed to give Stalin a free hand in Eastern Europe, and Russia promised to join the war against Japan once Germany had been defeated. Roosevelt, as can perhaps be seen here, was seriously ill and would die within three months.

With Josef Stalin, Moscow, 1942.

Churchill went to Moscow to meet Stalin, armed only with vague promises. The Allies were not yet ready to attack in the West, the war was going badly in North Africa and disastrously in the Far East. Nevertheless, there was a chemistry between the two men. The British and Russian leaders were both garrulous and fond of alcohol and, despite the smiles, they shrewdly assessed each other's characters. Stalin liked to irritate Churchill to test his reactions. Churchill used the bonhomie of these occasions to ask awkward questions, such as one about Stalin's destruction of the Kulak class (small independent farmers). Stalin's reply – 'We had to do it. What is a generation?' – must have chilled the emotional British premier.

Visiting an anti-aircraft battery, England, 1944.

The Churchills' three daughters were all in the armed forces. Mary, the youngest, belonged to an anti-aircraft gun crew. As this was situated in Kent, her parents made a visit from Chartwell. Her father was clearly delighted when the guns were brought into action against German V1 rockets.

Preparations for Overlord, England, 1944.

As troops gathered in southern England for the invasion of France, Churchill visited units, including his old regiment, the 4th Hussars, of which by now he was honorary Colonel. He had great faith in Montgomery, who had performed so well in the desert, though the self-indulgent Prime Minister could never quite bring himself to empathize with a non-smoker and tee-totaller. 'In retreat indomitable, in advance invincible, in victory insufferable,' was his private view.

Watching an artillery barrage from near the front line, Italy, 1944.

In the summer of 1943 the Allies invaded and captured Sicily. They then landed in Italy – bringing the war to the European mainland for the first time – and began a slow and costly advance up the peninsula.

Mussolini was deposed and Italy joined the Allies, but German forces stubbornly defended the territory of their recent partner, creating a defensive position – the Gothic Line – that proved extremely difficult to crack. Only after their homeland had been overrun did the German forces in Italy capitulate.

Though Churchill, like the majority of military planners, was much more concerned with Western Europe than the Italian 'sideshow', he visited the fighting there and had no qualms about going to the 'sharp end'. He watched British artillery firing while seated comfortably in the upstairs room of a villa.

Watching the fleet sail, England, 1944.

At a highly important moment for the man who had become Prime Minister just before the retreat from Dunkirk, Churchill views the vast fleet – the largest number of ships ever assembled before or since – that would take the Allied armies to Normandy. Britain was no longer friendless, as she had been in 1940. With two powerful allies and almost unlimited war material, he had every reason to think the defeat of Germany was inevitable.

Crossing to France, English Channel, 1944.

Churchill had been determined to sail with the invasion fleet, and would have loved to watch the naval bombardment of the beaches. Only a direct order from the King, who stated that since he himself was not allowed to go, his Prime Minister should not either, prevented Churchill from taking part in the adventure.

Arrival in France, Normandy, 1944.

Churchill crossed the Channel as soon as he could in the wake of the invasion, and came ashore dressed in his customary Royal Yacht Squadron rig. To land the vast amount of supplies, weapons and men necessary, he had encouraged the development and use of 'mulberries' – massive prefabricated concrete sections that formed an artificial harbour, which he can be seen clambering on to here.

Churchill at the front, Normandy, 1944.

Arrived in France and still in his nautical uniform, Churchill travelled by Army jeep into the hinterland. All around were the signs of recent fighting – wrecked buildings and vehicles, crashed gliders and aircraft, the corpses of men and of the red Normandy cattle that had grazed in the fields. He had a long-developed ability to shrug off battlefield horrors. He felt – and spread among the troops he met – a sense of cheerful optimism that the Great Crusade had at last begun its final phase. Nevertheless, heavy and costly fighting lay ahead before Normandy was liberated.

The Prime Minister on tour, Cherbourg, 1944.

Visiting the port city of Cherbourg, Churchill has a surprise encounter with one of the locals. The fact that he was a heavy smoker gave him an instant rapport with men of all types in all situations. His name had been well-known in occupied Europe (if only as a target of Nazi propaganda), and his presence with the liberating armies naturally aroused a great deal of curiosity. Despite the classless nature of this meeting, he is now travelling in a luxurious staff car.

Meeting troops at the roadside, Normandy, 1944.
Many Allied soldiers were startled to find the
premier among them in what was still a dangerous
area. He was very much in his element, addressing
groups of this kind as a combination of politician
and commander-in-chief.

With General Montgomery inspecting troops, Normandy, 1944.

Enjoying the opportunity to speak informally to soldiers who landed on D-Day, the Prime Minister no doubt thanked them for their efforts in the fighting.

Montgomery was a leader as colourful and inspiring as Churchill – if more austere. His charisma was expressed in his famous two-badge beret (a trademark worthy of the Prime Minister himself) and in his informal – even scruffy – version of military uniform. It would be difficult to imagine an American, let alone a German, commander dressing so casually.

In fact, this type of non-regulation dress had become commonplace, and acceptable, in the desert. The climate and the terrain had made spit and polish impractical, with sand everywhere and ferocious changes in temperature between day and night. Loose corduroy trousers and an ancient pullover would have made Montgomery look, to his men, not like a man bent on flouting military discipline but like the hardened, experienced North Africa veteran he was.

Free France, Paris, 1944.

The French capital was liberated in August, and a
few months later Churchill visited the city he had last
seen in 1939. Here he and his host, General de Gaulle,
inspect a guard of honour.

Reception from the French, Paris, 1944.

Throughout the Occupation, de Gaulle and Churchill had been symbols of hope for the French people. De Gaulle had been received in Paris after the liberation as a conquering hero. He was visibly irritated to find the British Prime Minister treated in the same way, but graciously acknowledged that without British assistance, Free France could not have survived. He made Churchill a Companion of the Liberation – a member of an exclusive order of resistance fighters that he had founded while in exile.

Churchill and Alexander, Italy, 1944.

Churchill visited every fighting front that was within reach. He is seen here with the Supreme Allied Commander Mediterranean, General Alexander. One of the most gifted and dynamic commanders of the war, Alexander had fought in the desert, in France with the BEF, and in Burma. He was an excellent choice for the difficult and bloody Italian campaign. In April 1945 he was to take the surrender of German forces in Italy. At over one million, this was the largest enemy force to capitulate during the war. Alexander went on to become Governor-General of Canada.

Following the advance into Germany, 1945.

At the end of 1944, Allied troops entered German
territory for the first time. By the beginning of the
following year they were moving over the frontier in
force. As always, the inquisitive Churchill visited the
scenes of recent fighting. Here he passes a wrecked
American Sherman tank in a German village.

At the Dragon's Teeth, Germany, 1945.

The western defences of Germany did not prevent
the Allied advance, and Churchill was soon able to see
this famous barrier for himself. This was another in the
series of symbolic moments that marked his journey
into the heart of the enemy's homeland.

In the front line, Germany, 1945.

When Allied forces crossed the Rhine in March 1945, the Prime Minister flew from London to witness the event. The enemy was still in the area, however; his visit to this bridge at Wesel had to be abandoned because artillery fire was being exchanged and several German shells landed nearby. The River Rhine was a natural barrier that had been fought over throughout history. For both sides it was of immense importance as the key to Germany, as it had the potential to slow down – and temporarily halt – the Allied drive into the heart of the country.

Infantry could, and did, get across. The east bank was secured by paratroops, but the movement of armour, supplies and larger bodies of troops required bridges, and it became a matter of urgency to capture one or more of these intact. The enemy, not unnaturally, wanted to prevent this at all costs. The bridge at Wesel was typical of many destroyed by the retreating Germans, and it was only by good fortune that another bridge, at Remagen, was captured. Once the enemy had been driven beyond the river the use of quickly assembled Bailey and pontoon bridges solved the problem.

At Hitler's bunker, Berlin, 1945.

Perhaps the most significant moment of the war for Churchill was this visit to his enemy's lair. Hitler's Chancellory, completed just before the outbreak of war, had been bombed almost to rubble, but the concrete bunker in which he had spent his last weeks defied destruction and remained intact. Churchill was shown the entrance to this by Russian troops. The chair he is examining would not have belonged to Hitler. It was probably placed in one of the corridors of the main building for those waiting for appointments with officials. Nevertheless it represented a good photo opportunity and Churchill obliged by sitting on the chair, to the amusement of his entourage.

The Big Three preside over the new Berlin, 1945.

Roosevelt, who had died in April, had been replaced by Harry Truman. The new President was expected to take over the massive US war effort in the last weeks of the European conflict. His face now appeared, with those of the other war leaders, on makeshift Russian monuments. Churchill too was about to vanish – not through death but by electoral defeat – and be replaced by an inexperienced successor.

It was clear by the last year of the war that the marriage of convenience between West and East – the Anglo-Americans and Russians – would not long outlive the defeat of Germany. Stalin had clearly decided on the rewards he intended to reap from the war (foremost being the occupation of as much of Europe as his forces could overrun) and would allow no consideration to deflect him from this.

Sullen suspicion and even hostility were evident almost as soon as the armies met. In the Soviet-occupied capital even Churchill experienced a measure of obstructiveness. In reality, the alliance dissolved as soon as Germany surrendered, but for a brief time a superficial solidarity prevailed. This monument in a Berlin park expresses that hollow camaraderie.

Opeming a leave centre for British troops,
Berlin, 1945.

Churchill, in Berlin for the Potsdam Conference
that was deciding the war's final phase, opened a
leave centre for British troops – named the 'Winston
Club' in his honour – on the Kurfürstendamm.

Leaving the Winston Club, Berlin, 1945.

Churchill was like a tourist on his visit to the enemy capital, constantly asking to visit buildings and monuments. The Russians, who occupied Berlin, were often uneasy and reluctant to let him wander unsupervised. He found – to his surprise – that the German inhabitants were more friendly than his own allies. Crowds followed him, cheered him, and tried to shake his hand. Small wonder that he said of the Germans, 'My hatred died with their surrender.'

Victory in Europe Day, London, 1945.

As the architect of Britain's victory, Churchill shared the moment of triumph with the Royal Family. He was given a rapturous ovation when, shortly afterwards, he appeared with Cabinet colleagues at a window in Whitehall and addressed the crowd. The war was not over – it was estimated that it would take another three years to defeat Japan, but at least the rebuilding of Europe could now begin. As part of that process, a general election was to take place.

Designing the post-war world with Truman and Stalin, Potsdam, 1945.

Though the wartime working relationship between the powers was already unravelling, enough remained of it to stage a final conference of the Allied leaders. It was decided to use the atomic bomb against Japan, and the future shape of Europe, with the Soviet sphere of influence, was confirmed. Germany itself was divided into zones of occupation administered by the four Allies. It was jocularly alleged that, in the carve-up of the country, the Russians got the agriculture, the British got the industry, the French got the fortresses and the Americans (whose zone included Bavaria) got the scenery. As wartime Prime Minister, Churchill had largely abandoned domestic concerns in order to pursue larger international issues. In the post-war world the voting public had other priorities and Churchill's party was seen as a less promising alternative. He was replaced as Prime Minister by Clement Attlee during the Potsdam conference.

The election of July 1945 was, for Churchill, a disaster. It gave Labour a majority of 180 seats in the Commons. Though genuinely admired by the British people as a wartime leader, it was clear to them that he could not meet the challenges of peace with the same ability. His opponents were preparing to establish the Welfare State and the National Health Service, and to address a critical housing shortage. The Conservative Party's only electioneering strategy was to boast that their leader was 'the greatest man on earth, the greatest statesman in the world.' This was, in fact, the problem. He was now a giant on the world stage and his attention was fixed on international issues, not on seemingly mundane domestic concerns. He had hoped to remain in power until the defeat of Japan had completed his work. In the event, he had abruptly to leave the conference in Potsdam at which he, Stalin and Truman were shaping the post-war world. Accustomed to the almost absolute power of a wartime premier, his sudden loss of office was a traumatic plunge into the depths. Though he put a brave face on his defeat, he felt he deserved better from the electorate.

Even at 70, Churchill was a man of consuming energy who could not bear inactivity. Having saved his country and ensured a heroic place in history, any further public life must surely seem an anticlimax. He was over retirement age, had memoirs to write and was as devoted as ever to painting. Clementine, who had privately believed that the strain of wartime leadership would prove too much and that he would die once the conflict was over, urged him to leave public life. This he would not consider. He remained Leader of the Opposition, unwilling to hand on the Conservative Party to a younger generation because he intended to win back the premiership.

In the meantime he had a great deal to do. He travelled through the once-occupied countries of Europe, and was showered with medals, honorary degrees and the freedom of cities. He began his lengthy history of the war as well as continuing another, interrupted literary project: his *History of the English-Speaking Peoples*. He was now the world's greatest celebrity and his writing could command enormous sums. The American magazine *Life* paid one and a half million dollars for the right to serialize it, and the *Daily Telegraph* offered half a million pounds. He became wealthy enough to add hundreds of acres to the Chartwell estate and to purchase two adjoining houses in Kensington. Despite having voted him out of office, the public greatly revered him (it had always been made clear by political commentators that there was nothing personal in their rejection of his party) and he was feted wherever he went.

This was true especially of the United States. Half-American by birth, he had been warmly welcomed there since his first visit in 1895, and held a deep affection for the country and its people. The American public cared little about his long career as a reactionary in British domestic politics, and overlooked his stubborn championing of the British Empire. For them, the war had made him a symbol of freedom that placed him on a level with Abraham Lincoln. And he was, after all, almost their own.

On a visit in March 1946, he made a speech at a college in Fulton, Missouri, about the new world order. The wartime truce in his dislike of Communism was decidedly over. He urged a robust response to the threat from Russia, and deplored the loss of so many great European cities behind what he called an 'Iron Curtain'. Though this phrase was not original – it had been used a year earlier by Goebbels – it was added to the list of his memorable sayings. His statements were forthright enough to cause some embarrassment (the British Government hastened to make clear that he had been expressing personal and not official views), but the level of interest in his opinions showed that he was still a statesman of considerable influence.

In October 1951, the post-war Labour government faced Churchill's Conservatives in another general election, and lost. At 77, he returned to Downing Street. During the following years his varied abilities would continue to command respect – it was agreeable to have a Prime Minister who won the Nobel Prize for Literature and whose horse won races and who sent in paintings to the Royal Academy Summer Exhibition. This time, however, there was little of the old fire in his premiership. He made no memorable speeches. He slept a good deal, and read novels. Though increasingly ineffectual he clung on to office, refusing to give in to old age or to his impatient successor, Anthony Eden.

As always since he had ascended the world stage, his interest was in international rather than domestic affairs. For much of his life he had been involved in war – training, planning, directing, or fighting it. Now that war might mean the end of civilization or even of humanity, however, he sought to become a peacemaker. Unable to halt the drive that impelled him towards fame and immortality, he wanted to set the seal on his career by arranging a disarmament summit, using his personal prestige to bring the sides together, and taking advantage of Stalin's death in 1953 to open a new chapter in East–West relations. This took place in Geneva, but neither Khruschev nor Eisenhower showed enthusiasm and it accomplished nothing. Mutual suspicion remained too deep.

The Empire was in terminal decline, though Britain made a gesture towards continuing greatness by detonating an atomic bomb. The European Community was born, in the shape of a Coal and Steel Union. On the other side of the world, the Korean War tested the resolve of the United Nations to act in concert against military aggression. At home, the Prime Minister threw himself enthusiastically into the organizing of the coronation, and when Queen Elizabeth II journeyed to Westminster Abbey in June 1953, he was allotted a carriage and an escort of hussars from his old regiment. He wore the uniform of Lord Warden of the Cinque Ports – yet another in his collection of splendid official costumes – but his health was precarious and he suffered a stroke only a few weeks later. There was to be a second of these the following year, shortly before his 80th birthday. In April 1955, he at last bowed to the inevitable, and resigned. He had defeated political opponents to win back office, but could not put up the same fight against old age.

On the campaign trail, London, 1945.

For the Prime Minister, it was something of an irritation to have to abandon the Potsdam Conference in order to campaign, but he threw himself into electioneering with his usual energy. He worried, however, that he had nothing new to say to voters.

Labour offered a dynamic and far-reaching programme that included nationalization of railways, coal and steel and the creation of a National Health Service. Churchill's greatness was his party's only election platform. It would prove insufficient.

He was a symbol of the old Britain. The voting public, wearied by the war, felt entitled to the benefits that were promised by his opponents and to the new Britain that these represented.

The edge of defeat, London, 1945.

Always a showman, Churchill put in a creditable performance in the election campaign, but the mood of many voters was disrespectful, if not openly hostile. Though he and his entourage felt they were headed for victory, something was not right.

Crucial in this election were the votes of service-men. Because so many of them were still overseas,

weeks passed before the result was known. It was a massive Conservative defeat. The disastrous election result came as a complete shock to Churchill, who was suddenly deprived of the trappings and the satisfaction of power. In public, he put a brave face on defeat. He paid tribute to the resilience of the British people and understood their desire for change and improvement. He even told a story – apparently true – of an old lady

in Athens who had asked: 'Poor Mr Churchill, I suppose now he will be shot?' In private, however, he felt the grip of despair, and refused to consider retiring from public life on such a low note. He remained at the helm of the Conservative Party and was still Leader of the Opposition, thus retaining an important place in politics and the opportunity to continue exerting some degree of influence on events.

Before speaking at the Congress of Europe,
The Hague, 1948.

Churchill had developed a strong belief in European unity, both as a means of preventing another war from breaking out among its component nations and as a bulwark against what had become the Eastern Bloc.

He addressed the Congress of Europe in May 1948 in words that were archetypally Churchillian: 'if we all pull together and pool the luck and the comradeship...then we shall move into a happier sunlit age, when all the little children now growing up may find themselves not the victors or the vanquished but the heirs of all

the treasures of the past and the masters of all the science, the abundance and the glories of the future.' Though dubbed on this occasion 'the first citizen of Europe', his interest in Europe was as a defensive alliance, not an economic community, and as premier he would take no practical steps towards integration.

At the lectern, Fulton, Missouri, 1946.

Though out of power, Churchill would never lose the prestige he had earned. He was now free to travel widely and received numerous invitations to speak. In March 1946 he delivered an address at Westminster College in Fulton, Missouri, in the company of President Truman. His theme was an old Churchillian one: the need for vigilance and military strength as a guarantee of peace for, as he remarked: 'From what I have seen of our Russian allies during the war I am convinced that there is nothing they admire so much as strength and nothing for which they have less respect than weakness.'

His stark and outspoken description of Cold War confrontation was perceived as alarmist during a period of *detente*, and the British Government dissociated itself from his remarks. Within a few years, however, the international climate had further cooled, and his assessment came to be seen as prophetic and realistic. His assertion that 'an Iron Curtain has descended across the Continent' was seen as a moment of seminal insight and the 'Iron Curtain speech' has become as enshrined in legend as his addresses of 1940.

On the bridge of the *Queen Elizabeth*, Atlantic, 1946

Churchill travelled to the United States on RMS *Queen Elizabeth* and, as the most important passenger on board, was invited to inspect the bridge. He had spent so much of his life dealing with maritime affairs that he would have found the experience familiar. The public's rejection of him at the polls had not been intended as ingratitude for his wartime leadership, and people everywhere wanted to show appreciation. He was treated with great kindness and found that, even more than in the past, his name would open doors – ensuring the best room in a hotel or the choicest table in a restaurant. As self-indulgent as ever, he had no difficulty in adapting to this.

Inspecting a guard of honour, Dover Castle, 1946.

Of the post-war honours offered to Churchill, few were as suited to his personality as the office of Lord Warden of the Cinque Ports. This ceremonial position – the titular protector of England's vulnerable coastline along the Straits of Dover – dates back to the 13th century and was once of considerable strategic importance. More recently the post had been held by William Pitt, the Duke of Wellington, Lord Salisbury and Churchill's friend Lord Curzon. It appealed to his romantic sense of history, and echoed his own role in protecting the same coast against more recent dangers. With the position came a gracious official residence, Walmer Castle, and a flamboyant uniform, which he wears here (with the sash of a Belgian order) as he inspects a guard of honour at Dover Castle.

Holidaying in Hendaye, France, 1945.

Shortly after the war in Europe ended, the Churchills took their first holiday since it had begun. By this time they were a valuable trophy for international photographers, and their appearance on a beach in the south of France attracted what would later be called 'paparazzi.' Interestingly, they seem to have made no effort to appear glamorous or even especially dignified. One of Churchill's most endearing qualities was his total absence of self-consciousness. He clearly did not mind being seen paddling with his trouser legs rolled up; all his life, there was something of the schoolboy about him. The couple were having a final walk on the beach before leaving for the Potsdam Conference.

Dressed for town, England, 1945.

In contrast to the image opposite, the Churchills were equally at home in formal situations and on official occasions. Clementine had feared that the strain of the war would prove fatal to her husband, and had hoped that – his ambition now sated – their lives could enter a quieter phase. He could not, however, have been happy away from the centre of great events. He had great literary projects to pursue and he still showed astonishing physical and mental vigour for a man of his age. There were to be no quiet years after all – at least not yet.

Speaking at the Conservative Party Conference, Brighton, 1948.

The once-hated Churchill had long since become the most revered Conservative of the century. His oratory style, which had stirred the nation in 1940 but had seemed overblown and somewhat pompous by the end of the war, had become a source of nostalgia – particularly since the Tories were now out of power.

His speaking style, a combination of grand phraseology and intimate conversation, captivated a new generation. He continued to give an impression of aloofness from prosaic domestic concerns and to project the image of an international giant rather than – like his opponent, Clement Attlee – that of an ordinary man aware of voters' concerns.

Conservative Party Conference at Liverpool
Stadium, 1951.

Churchill's emotional nature was entirely at odds
with his upper-class background, but could paradox-
ically be seen to reflect an aristocratic indifference
to the restraints of conventional behaviour. He wept
openly in many circumstances – when visiting
bombed areas, when reading reports of hardship
or atrocity, when receiving gifts or tributes, or –
as here – when given an ovation. His life involved
moments of greater elation and depression than
those of most people, but this year saw one of his
triumphs. His party defeated Labour and he once
again became Prime Minister. Having been perceived
as out of touch and old-fashioned, he had proved an
electoral asset once again.

El Alamein Reunion, London, 1952.

Churchill shared with Field Marshal Montgomery – a leader with similar qualities and an equivalent flair – the affection of many thousands of veterans. General Eisenhower held a similar place in the hearts of Americans. Here the three men attend an Alamein reunion at the Empress Hall in London's Earl's Court. Churchill, sporting an impressive medal collection, could boast more awards than most professional soldiers. He received a total of 33 British and foreign orders and medals, including the North Africa Star, the Italy Star and the France and Germany Star. He was undoubtedly an inspired war leader, but his ultimate success in Europe has not obscured his responsibility for terrible calamity elsewhere. He failed to ensure the adequate defence of Far Eastern territories, and the resulting loss of Singapore was the greatest military disaster in British history.

Cheered by the boys of his old school, Harrow, 1955.

Churchill had not been a keen Old Harrovian – as a radical young minister he had been booed on a visit to the school, and had not forgiven the boys. Harrow also had a grudge to bear: when asked to judge a reading competition following a lunch at which he had partaken too freely of the headmaster's hospitality, Churchill slept ostentatiously through the proceedings and, waking up, simply awarded the prizes in alphabetical order of the boys' surnames. During World War II he had, however, been impressed by the school's refusal to evacuate to a safer place, and from this regard a new relationship was born. He began to attend school events regularly, and became a frequent guest until old age prevented him.

Photographers record Churchill's arrival at
Buckingham Palace, London, 1952.

Churchill arrives at Buckingham Palace for the
proclamation of the death of King George VI on 6
February. His long career in public service had
accustomed him to dealing with such events. In 1910,
as Home Secretary, he had been one of the first
outside the Palace to be informed of the death of
Edward VII. Now, as Prime Minister, he was even more
closely concerned with the matter of the Succession.

Arriving for a meeting of the Air League,
London, c.1955

Churchill is surrounded by curious members of the
public as he arrives. As he was getting older, people
realized that any glimpse of him might be their last.
These children's parents seem to have encouraged
them to crowd in for a look at the great man.
Doubtless they will never have forgotten their
encounter. Churchill was once asked by a small
boy if he really was the greatest man in the whole
wide world. He snapped: 'Of course I'm the greatest
man in the whole wide world. Now buzz off.'

Winston and Clementine on the Pink Terrace,
Chartwell, c.1952

In the years following the end of World War II,
Churchill had turned his home and its grounds into a
fully developed country estate by adding 500 acres of
farmland and beginning livestock breeding. His son-in-
law, Christopher Soames, became estate manager. It
was intended that Chartwell should become an
ancestral home for Churchill's branch of the
Marlborough family – Blenheim Palace on a smaller
scale – but his son Randolph settled elsewhere. The
house boasted a small private cinema in which the
estate staff sometimes joined the family to watch
recently released films.

Leaving his town house, London, *c.*1955

Churchill's sizeable post-war earnings – as a writer he earned six-figure sums for serialization rights to his memoirs and other books – enabled him to purchase a London residence in addition to his country home. He bought two adjoining properties in Hyde Park Gate, a quiet side street opposite the park. One of these became his home, the other his office. Because he remained a Member of Parliament, he required a base in central London, but the house was too far from Westminster for convenience, and so he also rented a suite at the Savoy as his 'forward headquarters'. Here he could host lunches or have his traditional siesta.

Visiting his kangaroo at London Zoo, *c.*1955.

After the war, Churchill received gifts of creatures from all over the world. These included a lion cub, a leopard, a kiwi bird and a kangaroo. Almost all of them were passed on to the professional care of zoo-keepers (only one gift – black swans from Australia – found a home at Chartwell), but their owner maintained an interest in all of them, for Churchill was well known as an animal lover. The *Daily Mirror* reported that: 'Mr Churchill visited the London Zoo to see his white kangaroo, Digger, the only albino kangaroo in Europe.' Digger had been a present from the Australian Stockbreeders' Association.

Arriving at Westerham Church for the christening
of his grandson, 1952.

Churchill's youngest daughter, Mary, lived with her
husband Christopher Soames on the Chartwell estate.
As a result their children spent formative years close
to him and to Clementine. On the occasion of the
christening of Jeremy Soames in the parish church,
Churchill arrives with another grandson, Nicholas.

The baby's godfather, Field Marshal Viscount
Montgomery, can just be seen behind them. Churchill
had never been a churchgoer, and when at Chartwell
he stayed in bed while his wife and children attended
Sunday morning services. He had, however, a proper
respect for the role of Christianity in national and
family life, appreciating the solemnity of services
and the beauty of liturgical language.

At a shoot, Wales, 1933.

Churchill was quite capable of a cavalier disregard for the impression his appearance in public and in the press made. This photograph of him, dressed in practical outdoor garments for a shoot arranged by his friend the Duke of Westminster, was published in the society magazine *The Tatler*. In his youth he had been slovenly in dress – on one occasion, while riding in Hyde Park with his mother, he had been mistaken for her groom – and he remained somewhat careless all his life. The siren suits, slippers, dressing gowns and extraordinary hats in which he was often photographed are testimony to the eccentricity of his taste in clothing.

The Garter ceremony, Windsor, 1954.

By contrast, Churchill delighted in dressing up. His school and army uniforms had been followed by a wealth of other formal costumes: as a member of the Privy Council, Royal Yacht Squadron, Trinity House, and as university Chancellor and Lord Warden of the Cinque Ports. Perhaps the grandest of these were the robes of the Most Noble Order of the Garter. This had been founded in 1348, and he became a member in 1954 at the invitation of Queen Elizabeth II. Each year, in June, the Knights of the Garter have lunch at Windsor Castle, after which they walk in procession through the precincts to a service in St George's Chapel.

Attending a Thanksgiving service, St Paul's
Cathedral, London, 1953.

Shortly after the Queen's coronation the Churchills
attended a service of thanksgiving for the event at
St Paul's Cathedral. The Prime Minister had looked
forward immensely to his part in organizing the

ceremonies. He had seen four coronations and five
monarchs during his lifetime (Edward VIII was
not crowned). Like Princess Elizabeth's wedding
and the Festival of Britain a few years earlier,
the coronation was a boost to national morale
after the drab and dangerous war years.

Churchill proposes three cheers for the new Queen,
Westminster, 1953.

With his lifetime of political experience and considerable store of wisdom, Churchill was in a position to
offer useful guidance to the young sovereign. His
relationship with Queen Elizabeth was seen as
mirroring that of the young Queen Victoria and her first
Prime Minister, Lord Melbourne, over a century earlier.

Attending the coronation dressed in the uniform
of Lord Warden of the Cinque Ports, London, 1953.

The Prime Minister travelled in a carriage supplied by
the Royal Mews – the Queen's stables at Buckingham
Palace. This was escorted by mounted soldiers from his
old regiment, the 4th Hussars. Eight men were chosen,
and trained for weeks to reach perfection. They accompanied the Churchills' carriage to Westminster Abbey,
and afterwards returned with them to Downing Street.
One of them recalled: 'The Prime Minister invited the
Officer Commanding to bring his men to No 10
the following day, as he wished to have a drink with
"this fine body of men". Next day the escort was duly
presented to Sir Winston and Lady Churchill, and
received sherry and cigars. The latter are treasured
mementos of a very great occasion.'

The Prime Minister greets the Royal Family on their
return from an official visit abroad, London, 1954.

The Queen, Prince Charles, Princess Anne and
the Prime Minister awaited the return of the Queen
Mother from a visit to Canada and the United States.
One of the Premier's tasks, dictated by protocol, was
to be present on such occasions. Two years
earlier, King George VI had died while Princess
Elizabeth and the Duke of Edinburgh were abroad.
He and the heads of the other parties had had
to attend her arrival home from East Africa as
the new sovereign.

Hosting the Queen at his retirement party, Whitehall, 1955.

Two days before the Churchills departed from Downing Street for the last time, they received the honour of a visit from Her Majesty the Queen and Prince Philip. The press were on hand to record the Queen's departure at the end of the evening. The Prime Minister wore the sash of the Order of the Garter and, at his throat, the Order of Merit (an award that is in the personal gift of the sovereign). As a product of the Victorian era, he had been delighted by the return of the resonant phrase 'God Save the Queen' after an absence of half a century. He had entered Parliament at almost the moment Queen Victoria died, and had known every monarch since King Edward VII.

In the library at Hyde Park Gate, *c.*1955.

Writing took up a great deal of Churchill's time in the decade after the war. As before, he assembled a team of young historians to carry out the spadework for him. He said that he selected men of different political views in order to enjoy the arguments that he then provoked among them. The first volumes of his epic *History of the English-Speaking Peoples* were published in 1956, but by then he had already reached the summit of authorship – he had been awarded the Nobel Prize for Literature in 1953. The citation announced that he was honoured for 'his mastery of historical and biographical description as well as for brilliant oratory in defending exalted human values'.

The unveiling of his portrait by Graham Sutherland, Westminster, 1954.

To celebrate his 80th birthday in November 1954, Churchill's parliamentary colleagues made a present-ation to him in the splendid setting of Westminster Hall. Their gift was a specially commissioned portrait by the painter Graham Sutherland. The recipient was grateful for their kindness – he wept, as was habitual at a mo-ment of such emotion – but the picture was not seen again. It made its subject look ancient and exhausted, as though defeated by time, and lacking all the fire and majesty that had made this physically unimpressive man into a colossus of words and actions. Both the Churchills hated it, and after Clementine's death it was found to have been destroyed. Even without his momentous wartime achievements, his career would have merited these celebrations because of its length and variety. By that time he had served in Parliament for almost five and a half decades, had twice been Prime Minister and had held every Cabinet office except Foreign Secretary. Adding to his abilities as writer and artist and his competent, though often flawed, feel for military strategy, he emerged as the most versatile public figure in recent British history.

Churchill with Anthony Eden awaiting the arrival
of Eisenhower for a conference in Bermuda, 1953.

In his second term as premier, Churchill continued
to influence international affairs. Seen as a warmonger
in the 1920s, 30 years later he withdrew British troops
from Egypt and refused to send forces to help France's
lost cause in Indo-China. He also supported the
entry of Germany into NATO as an ally against the
Soviet threat and saw Britain acquire an atomic
bomb. His attempt to interest Eisenhower, at this
conference, in an East-West summit following
Stalin's death met with little enthusiasm.

Eden, a popular and efficient Foreign Secretary, was
universally regarded as Churchill's natural successor.
He was to wait an entire decade after the end of the
war to claim his inheritance, however.

The wedding of Churchill's niece to Anthony Eden, Whitehall, 1954.

Towards the end of Churchill's tenure in Downing Street, Anthony Eden – his Foreign Secretary and 'crown prince' – married the Prime Minister's niece, Clarissa Churchill, in a ceremony at Caxton Hall, Westminster. The couple were photographed afterwards in the garden of No 10, and outside the front door. Within a short time Clarissa, who was a daughter of Churchill's brother Jack, would be living in the house as the wife of the Prime Minister, though her tenure would be short. Her husband was to resign for health reasons in 1956 following the abortive Anglo-French occupation of the Suez Canal.

Churchill leaves Downing Street for the last time, Whitehall, 1955.

During his second term in office as Prime Minister Churchill had clung on to power – though he was clearly losing the ability to use it. He spent a good deal of his time reading novels, directing his literary projects, and travelling. Nevertheless his final exit from Downing Street was treated as the end of an era, and both press and public turned out in force to see him off. Before the street was closed to the public with the building of enormous gates in the 1980s, it was possible for the curious to go up to the front door in the hope of seeing the Prime Minister at close quarters. Here British and foreign press photographers wait for Sir Winston to appear.

Making his final departure, Whitehall, 1955.

The waiting press pack outside 10 Downing Street were rewarded when Sir Winston emerged, dressed in a formal frock coat, to travel to Buckingham Palace and tender his resignation.

This was yet another 'end of an era' – only six months after the celebration of his 80th birthday.

He was leaving the premiership but not politics, for he would continue to represent his constituency in Parliament. After the humiliation of his electoral defeat in 1945, he now had the satisfaction of quitting office voluntarily, leaving his chosen successor to carry on his policies. It must have been a satisfying feeling.

By the time he departed from Downing Street, Mr Churchill had become 'Sir Winston'. When World War II ended and his career seemed over, King George had offered to make him a duke – perhaps Duke of London. This had been declined, largely because Churchill wanted to remain in the Commons (Prime Minister was a title he coveted more). He was also asked if he would accept the Garter, Britain's oldest and highest order of knighthood. Though he undoubtedly deserved this, he was still smarting from electoral defeat, and had declined with the quip that he could hardly accept the Order of the Garter when the British people had just given him the Order of the Boot. Almost a decade later, when re-election had brightened his mood, he had accepted the Order from the new sovereign.

Once retired from the premiership he had little to do. Nevertheless his mind could not let go of the badges of office or the levers of power. He therefore remained MP for Woodford in Essex until 1964, nominally still involved in the business of government although he very seldom visited the Commons, where he was often unable to hear, or follow, proceedings.

He still travelled, and he continued to paint. He made a final visit to Washington and stayed with President Eisenhower at the White House. He spent long periods in the South of France,

staying – as he always had – with wealthy and indulgent friends. Such was the esteem in which he was held that his transport and hotels were often provided at no cost and Churchill, who all his life had combined a refusal to make do with second best and an often chronic lack of funds, had long since developed into an accomplished cadger. He had no qualms about inviting himself to stay, for weeks or months, at the villas or on the yachts of acquaintances (the Greek shipping magnate Aristotle Onassis was delighted to befriend Churchill, and invited him on several elaborate Mediterranean cruises). Day after day, the Great Man would sit for hours, smoking, dabbing at his canvases with a paintbrush (he was to continue painting until virtually the end of his life), talking or playing bezique. As with most elderly men, he had a number of regrets. He was deeply pessimistic about the international situation and viewed the future with terrible unease. Unashamedly nostalgic for the world into which he had been born – the Pax Britannica and the old European empires – he felt that he had saved civilization only for it to face extinction. All the things that had fascinated him about war – the genius of strategists, the valour and endurance of armies, the twists of fate and fortune that assisted victory or defeat – would be absent from conflict that would be decided by the push of a button. This prospect was a tragic end to a lifetime of service.

He continued to be the recipient of awards and honours. Such was his popularity in the United States that in 1963 he was created an honorary American citizen. This gesture had been made only once before in the nation's history, to recognize the contribution to independence of the Frenchman Lafayette. Churchill was too frail to travel to Washington for the ceremony, but his son Randolph represented him, receiving from President Kennedy – himself a lifelong admirer of Churchill – the specially created passport that proved his status.

Churchill was now not only an honorary American but a singularly privileged one. A few years earlier he had been installed as a member of the Society of the Cincinnati. Founded in 1783, membership is restricted to descendants of Revolutionary War officers. Churchill qualified through his mother, a New Yorker whose ancestor, Lieutenant Reuben Murray, had served in Connecticut. When invested with their badge, Churchill was told: 'Never has a recipient better shown his staunch courage and readiness ever to sacrifice things material for a principle.' Praise indeed, for George Washington had belonged to the Society. Membership has been described as America's equivalent of the Order of the Garter. Churchill, unique in this as in so much else, is the only man to have held both honours.

His own country also devised a unique means of recognizing him. Churchill had a lifelong interest in gadgetry and science, evidenced by his friendship with 'the Prof'– his technical adviser, Frederick Lindemann. One day, after leaving office, he was heard to regret that he had not done more to encourage young British scientists. He believed that Britain's future would depend on a continuing supply of trained technocrats. From this there developed the scheme to establish a college at Cambridge that would have a technical bias – a deliberate attempt to create a British equivalent of the American MIT. Churchill took a close

interest in the planning of the college. He gave £25,000 of his own money towards it, and ceremonially planted trees on the site. The public gave three and a half million pounds, and Churchill College was opened in 1964. Yet again Churchill defied convention, by being involved in choosing, planning and even paying towards his own national monument.

He was also concerned with another type of memorial. For some years he had been making plans for what he called 'Operation Hope Not'. This was his funeral, which he envisaged as a national spectacle, filled with pomp and pageant. When told of impending cuts in the armed forces, he was irritated by the notion that there would not be enough bands to play on the occasion, and expressed the hope that these economies would be postponed until afterwards.

His last years were a time of sadness and frustration. The old tireless energy was gone, but he found inactivity deeply irksome. The public largely lost touch with him, for he was seldom seen in the press except on his birthdays, photographed at the window of his house in Hyde Park Gate. He could only wait listlessly for the end. 'It's all so boring,' was his last recorded statement. He died, a few days after a major stroke, on 24 January 1965. His father had died on the same day, 70 years earlier.

His funeral was the sombre but splendid occasion he had hoped for. After a service at St Paul's, his body was taken by boat up the Thames to Waterloo Station, and then conveyed by train to Oxfordshire, where he was buried at Bladon. His was the only state funeral for a commoner granted in the 20th century. A most unusual honour for this most unusual of men.

With the trustees of Churchill College at Hyde Park Gate, London, 1958.

Despite his own lack of university training, Churchill knew the academic world. He had been Chancellor of Bristol University since 1929 and one of his closest associates and advisers, Frederick Lindemann, was an Oxford professor. Through Lindemann, Churchill's interest in science steadily grew, but only after leaving office did he come to regret that his government had not encouraged the training of technocrats and scientists. Lindemann suggested that Churchill's prestige could attract funds for the establishment of a college that would fulfil his dream, and this was quickly transformed into a scheme to make it a national tribute to him. With his customary enthusiasm, Churchill followed progress, donated a substantial amount of money – and even marked the site in Cambridge by planting two trees.

MR. JOHN HAY WHITNEY

MARSHAL of the RAF VISCOUNT PORTAL

MARSHAL of the RAF LORD TEDDER

LT-GEN. SIR BRIAN HORROCKS

GENERAL LORD ISMAY

FIELD-MARSHAL VISCOUNT MONTGOMERY

FIELD-MARSHAL VISCOUNT ALANBROOKE

SIR WINSTON CHURCHILL

PRESIDENT EISENHOWER

FIELD-MARSHAL EARL ALEXANDER

MR. HAROLD MACMILLAN

With President Eisenhower and other wartime leaders, London, 1959.

Churchill attended a reunion of wartime leaders held at Wingfield House, the London residence of the United States Ambassador, during an official visit to Britain by President Eisenhower. At 85, he was a generation older than the other attendees who had held positions of command in the Allied Armies. His relations with senior officers and military professionals had not always been this cordial. From the beginning of his career as a cavalry subaltern he had been critical of generals, and through his years as a self-assured politician and would-be warlord, to World War I and his military gambles, he had attracted a steady dislike. His conduct in the next war, however – above all the sense of unflinching purpose with which he pursued victory – had largely earned him the respect and devotion of those who carried out his orders.

The print was helpfully captioned by the newspaper picture department before its original publication.

On holiday with Aristotle Onassis, Greece, 1960.

In the last decade of his life Churchill spent several holidays with the Greek shipping millionaire, Aristotle Onassis. Churchill had always had close links with what had become known as the 'jet set.' A long-time visitor to Monte Carlo casinos and a veteran of cruises in the Mediterranean, he enjoyed the company of wealthy and rather colourful men. Clementine often disapproved of these friends and would have nothing to do with them. As a guest, her husband made himself at home amid the luxury that the rich could provide. Onassis regarded it as a great privilege to have Sir Winston as a friend, and made sure that he wanted for nothing when aboard his yacht, the *Christina*.

Visiting Venice, c.1960.

Churchill visiting the Grand Canal in a launch from the *Christina*, identifiable as always by his large cigar and one of the numerous sun hats or Stetsons that he acquired on his travels. His son Randolph once said: 'My father never met a hat he didn't like'. There was one exception however – Churchill hated the Glengarry bonnet he was expected to wear when serving with the Royal Scots Fusiliers during World War I, and adopted a French steel helmet instead. Hats had been a Churchill trademark since his childhood, and many of them are now preserved at Chartwell. As he became older and was more rarely seen in public, the images that appeared in the press increasingly showed a stooped and frail figure, wearing an enormous hat. The style became almost a symbol of his defiant refusal to yield his spirit to old age.

Welcome home, London Airport, 1959.

Returning from a visit with President Eisenhower, Churchill is greeted by Jane Montague Brown, the five-year-old daughter of his Private Secretary.

Churchill was an experienced air traveller. During the war he had had at his disposal a private aeroplane maintained and crewed by the Royal Air Force, and he had used this extensively for his journeys to attend conferences. The aircraft was cramped but comfortable, though travel over such great distances was exhausting and dangerous. General Douglas MacArthur later paid tribute to Churchill's courage in making these journeys: 'A flight of 10,000 miles through hostile and foreign skies may be the duty of young pilots, but for a statesman burdened with the world's cares it is an act of inspiring gallantry and valour.'

Greetings, London Airport, 1959.

When leaving for the same visit, he had met three small boys in sailor suits, and the encounter proved irresistible to a press photographer. The boys, who were the sons of Baron and Lady Hesketh, had been at the airport to greet their mother. In the second picture Churchill shakes hands with air hostess Kathleen Dyer. When departing or arriving, Churchill was frequently met by well-wishers. He also made a point of thanking the airline staff.

In peacetime, he resumed his habitual unpunctuality when travelling, and expected trains or aircraft to wait for him. When once asked why he seemed incapable of arriving in time to catch these, he replied that as a gambling man he wanted to give them a sporting chance to get away.

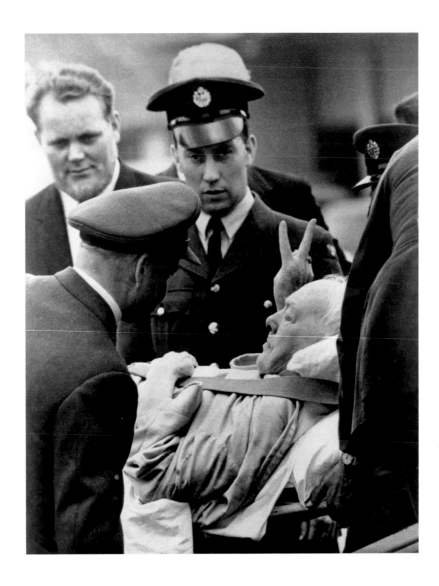

Arriving home for treatment at the Middlesex
Hospital for a broken thigh bone, London, 1962.

 As a sort of living national monument, Churchill's
health was a matter of concern to the public, and any
sudden change in his fortunes would cause a flutter
of interest. In August 1962, while on holiday in Monte
Carlo, he broke his thigh bone. He returned to the
United Kingdom for treatment, and is seen here
entering the Middlesex Hospital. Always comfortable under the public gaze, he was quite capable
of displaying all his old resilience and humour,
flashing the customary V-sign.

Leaving the Middlesex Hospital in fine fettle, London, 1962.

Newspaper readers were accustomed to the sight of Churchill going in and out of hospital. In 1932 he had contracted paratyphoid fever and had been pictured in the press being carried on a stretcher into a London nursing home … and cheerfully smoking when carried out. The previous year he had suffered an even greater misfortune. While visiting the United States on a lecture tour, he had been knocked down by a taxi while crossing Fifth Avenue. Hospitalized with fairly serious injuries, he not only received a visit from the unfortunate cab driver, but wrote an article about his accident that earned him the equivalent of £600 – enough to pay for a recuperative holiday in the West Indies.

Addressing constituents of Woodford, Essex, 1959.

Churchill addressed his Essex constituents in April
1959 on the situation in Europe. He had not given a
speech in public for two years, and read this one aloud
from notes – a far cry from the oratorical flourish of
his earlier days.

Being helped to his feet by Christopher Soames at the same event, Essex, 1959.

As a newspaper reported: 'He told a large audience in the Sir James Hawkey Hall that the West cannot abandon West Germany or West Berlin. The 84-year-old former Premier also said he intended to stand for re-election to Parliament. Then he dashed away to attend a division in the House of Commons.' The word 'dash' seems hardly appropriate, given the difficulty that the speaker clearly had in rising from his seat. He is seen here being assisted by Christopher Soames (at left), who was married to his daughter Mary, and had served as his Parliamentary Private Secretary from 1952–55. Churchill, though preoccupied for much of his career with wider issues, was a conscientious MP who remained popular with his constituents. He is known to have kept supplies of brandy, champagne and cigars at a local hotel for use when he was in the area.

Sitting for a photograph to mark the award of honorary citizenship of the United States, London, 1963.

Half American by birth, Churchill became a fully fledged – but honorary – citizen of the United States when he was presented with the document by Ambassador David Bruce at his home in Hyde Park Gate. It was signed by President John F. Kennedy, who had admired Churchill's writing style since he was a college student, and who had said of the former Premier's wartime speeches: 'He mobilized the English language and sent it into battle.' Too frail to attend the White House ceremony at which the honour was bestowed, Churchill was represented by his son. Though the honour has been posthumously bestowed upon four other worthies, Mother Teresa was the only other recipient of the accolade during her lifetime.

The retired leader, London, *c*.1960.

In old age Churchill, comfortable with his achievements and his long record of service, had a benign and avuncular appearance that contrasted with the driven and anxious look he wore in some younger portraits. This photograph suggests the mischievous, puckish humour for which he was known. Although his wit and humour delighted Parliament and public for over half a century, he was subject all his life to depression, or 'black dog' as he called it. Near the end of his life the cause of his greatest melancholy was the thought that, as he put it, 'I have achieved a great deal to achieve nothing in the end' – he feared that all he had fought for could be annihilated by another, final war.

Churchill painting the village of Camara de Lobos, Madeira, 1950s.

Churchill's paintings were a solace in old age because they enabled him both to work and to rest at the same time. Seated comfortably at his easel and with his bodyguard to shoo away any curious local children, he could lose himself for hours. He painted mostly landscapes, though his renderings of people were usually creditable. His use of colours was bold, and he rendered to good effect the play of shadow and the glimmer of sunlight on water. As with so much else about him, his light-hearted hobby had a serious purpose – the relief of stress and depression. This spot is now marked by a plaque.

Attending a private view at the Royal Academy, London, c.1958.

Churchill enjoyed his connection with the Royal Academy – in 1948 he was elected 'Honorary Royal Academician Extraordinary'. This entitled him to attend their annual dinner and to 'send in', or hang, six paintings a year in the Summer Exhibition. Here he talks at a private view to Charles Wheeler, a distinguished journalist and art connoisseur. Churchill was unimpressed by modern art but was always eager to talk to other painters and to learn from their styles and techniques. Many of them respected his talent. Sir John Rothenstein said of him that, if he had devoted himself seriously to painting instead of pursuing other endeavours, 'he would have painted big pictures', meaning that he could have been a major artist.

French President Charles de Gaulle leaving Churchill's London house after a visit, 1964.

Churchill and de Gaulle had been wartime associates, but not friends. Nevertheless they had a great deal in common – both had struggled to save their countries in 1940 and both had had a firm conviction that only they could do so. Both had known derision, unpopularity and rejection, both had travelled from a place of exile on the fringe of poliltical life to attain the highest offices of state available to them.

De Gaulle's arrival at Hyde Park Gate with his wife, while on an official visit to London in 1964, was prompted by a combination of protocol and personal respect. The great elder statesman merited the homage of visiting dignitaries but de Gaulle also nursed memories of his years as a fugitive in London. Churchill had backed him rather than any other would-be French leader and had thus put him on the road to power and national recovery. However loath the French President may have been to acknowledge this, it was a debt that had to be honoured.

Churchill at his front door after a visit by the Crown Prince of Morocco, London, 1960.

Like many great men, Churchill became something of a tourist attraction. Heads of state, politicians, plutocrats and intellectuals would often, when visiting London, want to call at his house in Hyde Park Gate – to exchange words, present gifts, or have a photograph taken with him. From Churchill's point of view these guests were usually welcome; they brought news and opinions from a world that was becoming increasingly remote.

The Crown Prince of Morocco was one such visitor. For Churchill, the Crown Prince's country was associated primarily with painting. Though Churchill was a largely self-taught artist, he had mastered the ability to capture the essence of a landscape, its shapes and tones, and he was particularly fond of working in the North African light. His paintings of the city of Marrakesh and of the Atlas Mountains are some of the best he produced.

His acquaintance with the region dated largely from his wartime visits, when the stress of events might be broken by a quiet hour with his paintbrush. In later, more peaceful times he loved it just as much.

Arriving at Parliament for his farewell speech
in the House of Commons, 1964.

At almost 90, Churchill maintained a sketchy
attachment to his old routine. He continued as a
Member of Parliament until September 1964 – though
he visited the Commons increasingly rarely – and
he kept abreast of important developments.

Enjoying a cigar, London, 1964.

To the public, Churchill was unimaginable without a cigar. His addiction had begun during his visit to Cuba in 1895, and he carried on smoking until his death. Though he constantly had a cigar in his mouth, he seldom inhaled, and he might hold one in his teeth for long periods without even lighting it if he were thinking deeply. Nevertheless, his consumption of them was impressive. He is thought to have worked his way through 4,000 cigars a year, which meant a quarter of a million during his life. His intake of alcohol was equally legendary. His scientific adviser, Professor Lindemann, worked out at dinner one evening how much champagne Churchill had drunk in his lifetime. The answer was: enough to fill a railway carriage. He drank this with meals, and liked to have a glass of whisky at his elbow during the rest of the day. This was always heavily diluted, however.

At a pantomime starring Sarah Churchill,
London, 1958.

   Churchill's second daughter, Sarah, became an
actress and dancer, appearing on the West End stage,
on Broadway and in Hollywood. In 1951 she co-starred
with Fred Astaire in the film *Royal Wedding*, but her
career did not reach any further heights. She had

married, in spite of her parents' strong disapproval, Vic
Oliver – an Austrian-American comedian 18 years her
senior, who became Churchill's particular *bête noire*
(not least because he earned on the stage twice as
much as his father-in-law did as Prime Minister!). The
marriage did not last, and tragically Sarah descended
into a life of alcoholism and depression.

She appeared, at Christmas 1958, in the title role in a
production of *Peter Pan* at La Scala Theatre in London.
Her parents visited her after the performance, and are
seen here with their grandchildren Emma and Jeremy
Soames, their daughter Mary's children. Also present is
Julia Lockwood (daughter of the actress Margaret) who
played Wendy.

Making his final public appearance, London, 1964.

Churchill's continuing presence in public life until his 80s was not merely a struggle against advancing age but also against failing health. He had suffered two strokes during the 1950s, and had shown all his customary toughness in carrying on in spite of them. By his 90th birthday, on 30 November 1964, he was no longer able to leave his home. He received more than 70,000 messages of congratulations from all over the world. He spent the day in bed, but made a fleeting appearance at a ground-floor window of his house in Hyde Park Gate to acknowledge the presence of a small and persistent crowd of well-wishers outside. This brief glimpse was the last that the public were to have of him. He was clearly waiting, as one of his daughters was to put it, 'with increasing patience and courtesy for the end,' and this was not long in coming. The following January, another stroke led to a coma. For nine days he lay unconscious while, once again, a crowd waited outside. On 24 January 1965, he died.

Lying in state, Westminster, 1965.

Churchill lay in state for three days in Westminster Hall, the vast medieval core of the Palace of Westminster. The scene of coronation banquets and of the trial of Charles I, it is a place of immeasurable historical and emotional significance for the English. Churchill had been well aware of this, for he had witnessed a more recent chapter in its history – the damaging by incendiary bombs of its great hammer-beam roof in 1941. Over the three days, 4,000 people passed his coffin every hour for 23 hours. 'It's not such a good lying-in-state as Edward VII's,' said an old lady, 'but nothing is as good as it was then.' Churchill, who always retained a sentimental attachment to the world of his youth, might have agreed.

Memorial service at St Paul's Cathedral,
London, 1965.

Six days after his death, Churchill's coffin was taken
in procession to St Paul's Cathedral, where a memorial
service was held. As well as the British Royal Family
there were the monarchs of Norway, Denmark,
Belgium and the Netherlands, the Grand Duke of
Luxembourg, the Presidents of France (Charles de
Gaulle) and Israel, former President Eisenhower,
Marshal Konev, and 16 prime ministers; there were
royalty and heads of state from 116 countries. The
coffin, which had been made from oaks cut on the
Blenheim estate, was adorned with the Order of the
Garter. The service included the singing of the 'Battle
Hymn of the Republic' in tribute to his American
parentage and his status as a symbol of freedom.

The funeral procession passes along Fleet Street
on its way to St Paul's, London, 1965.

Churchill's connection with all three of the armed
services was emphasized by the units taking part.
Members of the Royal Air Force Regiment accompanied the bier with arms reversed. His orders and

medals were carried by officers of his old regiment,
now called the Queen's Royal Irish Hussars. The gun
carriage was pulled by sailors, though this is in fact
traditional at British state funerals. The custom began
with the burial of Queen Victoria in January 1901,
when the horses pulling the gun carriage were unable

to make headway on slippery cobbles. They were
unhitched and the naval guard of honour was ordered
to step in and seize the traces. The ratings performed
so well, and looked so impressive, that they have
performed the duty ever since. More than 7,000 service
personnel took part in Churchill's funeral procession.

Paying final respects, London, 1965.

Following the service, the coffin was once again loaded on to its carriage. As the Royal Family and the congregation watched, it was taken in procession towards the Tower of London where, at Tower Pier, it was transferred to a Port of London Authority launch, *Havengore*. This bore Sir Winston upstream towards Festival Pier. A 17-gun salute was fired and RAF Lightnings flew overhead. In what was perhaps the most memorable image of the day, the dockland cranes that lined the river's south bank bowed as the coffin passed. At Festival Pier, it was borne by Guardsmen to nearby Waterloo Station where a train, pulled by the locomotive *Sir Winston Churchill*, waited to take it home to Blenheim. The streets were filled with people, mostly silent, conscious that they were witnessing a moment of national drama and solemnity that might never be equalled in their lifetimes.

A memorial statue makes its way to Kent,
London, 1969.

Churchill lived on in the public consciousness as
statues of him began to appear throughout Britain
and the world. This one, destined for Westerham –
the village nearest his home in Kent – would become
familiar to generations of visitors to Chartwell.

Lady Churchill unveiling a statue of her husband in the Members' Lobby of the House of Commons, London, 1969.

This sculpture, by Oscar Nemon, is one of two statues that commemorate Churchill in the neighbourhood of the Palace of Westminster; the other is outside in Parliament Square, facing Palace Yard. Elsewhere within the capital, there is a seated bronze statue of him – also by Oscar Nemon – in the Guildhall and a more curious monument in Old Bond Street: this, entitled *Allies*, is a pair of bronze figures – Churchill and Roosevelt – seated on a wooden park bench and apparently engaged in light-hearted conversation.

Other memorials have included a lecture theatre at the Royal Military College, a college at Cambridge, an international scholarship, and a host of streets. Several museums, libraries and collections celebrate his life and achievements. One of these is beneath Whitehall in London, and includes the complex of underground rooms from which he directed Britain's war effort.

CHRONOLOGY

1874, Nov 30 Born at Blenheim Palace.

1886 Winston's father Lord Randolph Churchill appointed Chancellor of the Exchequer, but resigned shortly afterwards.

1888 Arrived at Harrow School.

1892 Left Harrow to attend an army 'crammer'.

1893 Entered Royal Military College, Sandhurst at 3rd attempt.

1894 Passed out of Sandhurst.

1895 Death of Lord Randolph Churchill. Commissioned into 4th Hussars.

1895, Nov–Dec Went to Cuba to observe Spanish forces, wrote articles for *Morning Post*.

1896 Departed for garrison duty in India with 4th Hussars.

1897, Sep Joined Malakand Field Force on India's North-West Frontier as correspondent, also served as officer.

1898 Joined expedition to Sudan, commanded by Kitchener, to defeat the Khalifa.

1898, Sep Battle of Omdurman. Churchill took part in cavalry charge by 21st Lancers; publication of *The Malakand Field Force*.

1899 Resigned commission. Returned to England.

1899, July Stood unsuccessfully for election as MP in Oldham, Lancashire.

1899, Oct Sent as newspaper correspondent to South Africa where war had broken out between Britain and Boer republics.

1899, Nov Published *The River War*.

1899, Nov 15 Armoured train ambushed by Boers. Churchill captured.

1899, Dec 12–23 Escaped from prison camp in Pretoria – made international headlines.

1900 Commissioned in South African Light Horse (unpaid) while remaining correspondent.

1900, Jan 20–22 Battle of Spion Kop.

1900, May Published first volume of Boer War history: *London to Ladysmith via Pretoria*.

1900, June Entered Pretoria with British troops. Liberated his former prison camp.

1900, July Arrived in England.

1900, Oct Elected MP for Oldham. Published Second volume of war history, *Ian Hamilton's March*.

1900, Dec Made lecture tours of Britain and North America.

1901, Jan Entered Parliament.

1904, May Switched allegiance from Conservative to Liberal Party.

1906 Published two-volume biography of Lord Randolph. Became Undersecretary of State for the Colonies.

1906, Sep Visited German army manoeuvres.

1908 Published *My African Journey*.

1908 Elected Liberal MP for Dundee.

1909, Sep Revisited German manoeuvres.

1910, Jan Appointed Home Secretary.

1911, Jan 'Battle of Sidney Street'; supervised soldiers and police while attending siege of anarchists' lair.

1911, Aug Sent for troops to deal with striking railwaymen.

1911, Aug Joined Committee of Imperial Defence. Wrote memo predicting the course of events in a future European war.

1911, Oct 25 Appointed First Lord of the Admiralty.

1912 Established Royal Naval Air Service.

1914, June Britain bought control of Persian oil for the Royal Navy at Churchill's urging.

1914, Aug 4 Britain declared war on Germany.

1914, Oct Assumed personal command of Allied troops defending Antwerp.

1915, Jan Proposed attack on Turkey to relieve pressure on Russia.

1915, Apr 25 Allied landings on Gallipoli peninsula.

1915, May 26 Coalition Government formed. Churchill appointed Chancellor of the Duchy of Lancaster.

1915, Nov 11 Resigned from the Cabinet. Went to France to serve in the Army as major.

1915, Nov–Dec Spent one month on Western Front with Grenadier Guards, then promoted to lieutenant colonel

commanding 6th Battalion, Royal Scots Fusiliers.

1916, May With amalgamation of battalions, lost post in Royal Scots Fusiliers; returned to England.

1917, July Became Minister of Munitions.

1918, Nov 11 War ended with armistice.

1919 Appointed Secretary of State for War and Minister for Air; responsible for demobilization.

1919, June 28 Peace settlement finalized at Versailles.

1922 Lloyd George's Government defeated. Churchill resigned as Colonial Secretary.

1923, Apr Published the first volume of *The World Crisis*, his personal history of World War I (completed 1931).

1924, Oct Churchill elected MP for Epping as Constitutionalist (quasi-Conservative).

1924, Nov As full Conservative, appointed Chancellor of the Exchequer.

1930, Oct Published memoir *My Early Life*.

1931 Resigned from Shadow Cabinet.

1931 Coalition Government led by Ramsay MacDonald. Churchill objected to their disarmament policy. Began his warnings regarding German re-armament.

1933, Aug Made major speech about German threat.

1933, Oct Published first volume of biography of Duke of Marlborough (completed 1936); Churchill predicted that

Germany's still-secret air force would equal the RAF in size by 1935.

1935 Joined Committee of Imperial Defence on Air Defence Research.

1938, Sept Neville Chamberlain signed Munich Agreement on behalf of Britain.

1939, Sep 1 German invasion of Poland.

1939, Sep 3 Britain declared war on Germany. Churchill appointed First Lord of the Admiralty.

1940, Apr Became President of the Military Co-ordination Committee.

1940, Apr 9 German invasion of Norway and Denmark.

1940, Apr Narvik operation – British attempt to forestall German capture of vital Norwegian port. Chamberlain, as Prime Minister, blamed for failure.

1940, May Chamberlain resigned following vote of no confidence.

1940, May 10 Germany invaded France, Netherlands, Belgium and Luxembourg. Churchill invited by King George VI to form a Government.

1940, May 13 Churchill delivered 'blood, toil, tears and sweat' speech.

1940, May 15 Britain loaned by USA 50 ancient destroyers.

1940, May–June 4 Dunkirk evacuation.

1940, June To bolster French resistance to Hitler, Churchill offered confederation that would pool sovereignty between Britain and France. This concept rejected by the French Government.

1940, July 4 Churchill ordered Royal Navy to bombard French fleet in the harbour at Oran to prevent its use against Britain. This impressed Roosevelt but made an implacable enemy of Vichy France, with serious consequences.

1940, Aug 20 Speech praising 'the few' – RAF fighter pilots – for their resistance to the Luftwaffe.

1940, Sep Beginning of the 'Blitz'.

1940, Oct Became leader of the Conservative Party.

1940, Dec Lend-lease Bill passed by US Congress.

1941, Mar British troops dispatched to Greece following German invasion.

1941, Jun 22 German armies invaded the Soviet Union. Britain and Russia become allies.

1941, Aug 12 Signing of Atlantic Charter, detailing war aims.

1941, Dec 7 Japanese attack on Pearl Harbor. US entered war.

1942, Feb 15 Fall of Singapore.

1942, Aug 2 Travelled to North Africa.

1942, Aug 12 Met Stalin in Moscow.

1943, Jan 12 Casablanca Conference with Roosevelt and French representatives. Agreement to demand unconditional surrender of Germany.

1943, May Visited Washington.

1943, Aug Quebec Conference.

1943, Nov Cairo and Tehran Conferences.

1943, Dec Fell ill with pneumonia.

1944, June 6 D-Day. Allied invasion of Europe.

1944, Aug 24 Paris liberated.

1944, Sep Second Quebec Conference.

1944, Oct Met Stalin in Moscow.

1944, Dec British troops intervened in fighting in Greece
(civil war).

1944, Dec 24 Went to Athens to negotiate a peaceful settlement
of the conflict.

1945, Feb Yalta Conference.

1945, Apr 12 Death of Franklin Roosevelt.

1945, May 8 Unconditional surrender of Germany ('VE Day').

1945, May 23 Resigned as Premier. End of wartime coalition.
Acted as 'caretaker' pending General Election.

1945, July 17 Potsdam Conference attended by President
Truman. Decision taken to use atomic bomb against Japan.

1945, July 26 General Election resulting in major defeat for
Conservatives. Churchill out of office, became Leader of the
Opposition.

1945, Aug 6 & 9 Atom bombs dropped on Hiroshima and
Nagasaki.

1945, Aug 15 Surrender of Japan ('VJ Day')

1946, Mar 'Iron Curtain' speech delivered at Fulton, Missouri.

1948, Jan Published first volume of *History of the Second World
War* (completed 1954).

1949, Mar North Atlantic Treaty Organization established.

1951, Oct 26 General Election. Churchill again Prime Minister
after Conservative win.

1952, Feb 6 Death of King George VI.

1952, Oct 3 First British atomic bomb exploded.

1953, Apr 24 Created Sir Winston Churchill, Knight of the Garter.

1953, June 23 Suffered mild stroke.

1953, Oct 15 Received Nobel Prize for Literature.

1954, Nov Second stroke.

1954, Nov 30 80th birthday.

1955, Apr 5 Resigned premiership.

1956, Apr Published first two volumes of *History of the
English-Speaking Peoples*.

1963, Apr 9 Created honorary US citizen.

1964, Sep Retired from Parliament.

1964, Nov 30 90th birthday.

1965, Jan 24 Died.

1965, Jan 30 State funeral.

PICTURE SOURCES

The images within the book have been selected principally from the archives of Mirrorpix, a unique resource drawing on the collections not just of the world famous *Daily Mirror* newspaper but also those of sister titles the *Daily Herald*, *Sunday Mirror*, *The People*, the *Daily Record* and *Sunday Mail*.

The *Daily Mirror* was first published in 1903 as a journal for women. After initial success, sales declined and the owner, Alfred Harmsworth, took the bold decision to print photographs as an additional means of conveying the news. With this innovation the age of photojournalism was born and the new illustrated pictorial *Daily Mirror* became the first newspaper in the world to publish photography. The *Daily Record* and the *Daily Herald* were also of early foundation, established in 1895 and 1912 respectively and both making extensive use of photography once the *Mirror* had shown the way. The newspapers' picture archives contain a wealth of material on Churchill, his life being uniquely well photographed, as a notable public figure from before the beginning of the 20th century until the end of his life in 1965. For every picture that was printed in the newspaper at the time, the archive contains many that weren't and consequently a number of photographs are published here for the first time.

All images copyright © Mirrorpix except: p12 document extract kindly supplied by Harrow School. pp17, 38, 46, 47, 50, 55, 158, 174, © Hulton Archive/Getty Images; p51 © General Photographic Agency/Getty Images; p54 © W.G. Phillips/Getty Images; pp79, 80, 94,168 © Time Life Pictures/Getty Images; pp82, 177 © Keystone/Getty Images; pp134, 135 © Fred Ramage/Getty Images; p145 © George Skadding/Time Life Pictures/Getty Images; p146 © Sam Shere/Time Life Pictures/Getty Images; p147 © Douglas Miller/Getty Images; p199 © Dennis Oulds/Getty Images.

ACKNOWLEDGMENTS

I gratefully acknowledge the assistance of John Mead and Lisa Rayman at Mirrorpix, the *Daily Mirror*'s picture archive in Watford, as well as the help of Allen Packwood, Sandra Marsh and Ieuan Hopkins at the Churchill Archives Centre, Churchill College, Cambridge. I would also like to thank Neil Baber and Ame Verso at David & Charles; Beverley Jollands for proofreading; Eileen Slatter for help in an emergency and Rita Boswell, archivist of Harrow School, for kindly providing the picture of the school's entrance register. Lastly, I thank – as always – my wife Sarah.